Ways Throu

WAYS THROUGH

Tony Holden

EPWORTH PRESS

British Library Cataloguing in Publication Data

Holden, Tony
Ways through.
1. Christian life. Spirituality
I. Title
248.4

ISBN 0-7162-0469-X

First published 1990
by Epworth Press
1 Central Buildings
Westminster, London SW1H 9NR

Typeset by Gloucester Typesetting Services,
Stonehouse, Glos.
Printed in England by
Clays Ltd, St Ives plc

*For Adam and Siân
and all our children's children . . .*

Contents

Part Three: How?

Important and Precious

1 The main point of it

I want to show you something of my life as a Christian. I want to do this in a very personal way. I want to describe my life on the basis of those things which actually happen to me and which form my life. I want to root this account in the situation and context within which I live. It will be an uneven journey, with detours, stops, wrong connections, breakdowns. But it will also, I hope, find some ways through to a way of living which is both human and Christian.

2 Children

When I was a child playing adventures on the streets and on the fields of my northern home, like millions of others, I belonged to a gang. Above all, more than the cricket and football on endless summer days, or our collective fear of the ghost which was said to have been seen in the window of an empty house, I remember huddling together in a small hut or within some bushes. We were always planning. Always we were making and agreeing, or more often not agreeing, the rules for the next game. Then came the moment for action. Out we went into the race or against the enemy, running hard. Sometimes, and I am sure I exaggerate, I found myself streaming ahead, running for all I was worth, only to find that the others had gone back to argue, again, about the ground rules.

We all join in games, institutions, history, societies when they are already in progress. We join in part way through when arguments have already taken place about the ground rules and when

some of the action is already past. We join in our own lives at a
specific time, a particular place and situation, and within an acutely
finite context. We do so in such a way that we are always involved
both in trying to discern the rules and to be part of the process of
making new rules up. In a sense we spend a great deal of our lives
trying to catch up on an understanding of what has been happening
in our time and place. We need to know something of where we
come from and where we are as a means of finding out who we
are. Our development from childhood to adulthood, our self-
consciousness and our ability to articulate something of the par-
ticularness of our time and place are bound up together.

Maybe there was a time when this process was worked out in
one time and place and from within one monochrome and unchanging view of the world. But if there was such a time it has
certainly gone from our British society. Here there are many views
of the world. Here the rules and indeed the games are constantly
changing. Here, as one novelist said, 'life is a public performance
on the violin in which you must learn the instrument as you go
along'. Having lived for many years with someone learning the
violin, I take this as a fairly demanding prospect!

When our twins were very little, I, like I am sure every other
parent, used to read stories to them or even make up stories for
them. For a time stories seemed to meet every need. There were
the classic ones, new ones on television, invented ones about 'Fred
the dinosaur' or whatever. At a later point there came questions
about the ultimates and absolutes of life. These searching questions, which probed for meaning and sense, were delivered with a
surprising directness and with, what felt like, a ferocity. They
came, to use cricketing terms, head high like a bouncer or decep-
tively low and fast. Yet it still seemed possible to care enough and
love enough to want to give proper answers. By proper I mean as
truthful as I could make them looking the questioner in the eyes.
Of course, part of the properness was to do with doubts, with not
knowing some of the answers, and with fears. I kept striving to
answer in ways which were sensible and creative. They were conversations whose emotion I shall not forget.

It was really through these conversations and experiences with
our young children that I began to search, more actively than I
had done before, for what is important and precious to me. I have

tried many times, especially over the last decade and as they have grown up into their teenage years, to set down those things that are important and precious to me. I feel that I do not want them only to hear a partial, unorganized or even public version of it. I am sure that all parents strive to pass on to their children the things they value. In some situations that means finding enough food to prevent them starving. In others it involves getting sufficient money to buy the basic necessities and pay the bills of a consumer society. But part of being a parent, for good and ill, is surely to do with trying to share what matters to you. You may do it clumsily, badly, even destructively but I am sure you do it. Years of being a parent and years of child rearing, in all their wonder, excitement, hard work, frustration, fear and loving, are not lightly set aside.

So I have tried both to understand for myself, and to set down for them, what is important and precious to me. What I am writing is in one sense a long and extended letter to them. I think my desire to share with them is what is motivating me. I think the prospect of them reading it and talking with me about it is what makes me aim, as hard as I can, to be truthful and to resist some of the more traditional answers and ideas which come to mind. In this important sense it is for them. But of course, in addition to my own need to write it, it is also for other people whose lives and journeys are sufficiently similar for them to recognize what I am struggling to express. I hope they also will find things in it to value.

3 Writing

I have tried many times to set all this down. I have tried in drawings, poems, articles, sermons, Bible studies, notes, and conversations. For much of the time what I want to say slips away from me. It goes out of focus or is lost through distractions and interruptions. Occasionally I stumble across what I want to say with an immediacy which comes out in a few pages of writing, a drawing or a poem. Usually it feels as though I have to gather together all my outreaching energies and breathe them into myself so as to form some centre out of which I can write.

So it matters to me a great deal that I should set this down, that I should, moreover, set it down in the way I want. It is important

because the words and writing them has always been an integral
part of the experience and the process. They have been persistent
as I have tried to write them down and as they have tracked within
my head in constant conversation.

It is strange that the need persists because I do find it so difficult
to write. I can go from confidence to a total inability to write in
minutes! Over the years I have been fascinated by the work of
creative people such as artists, film makers, writers. I often find
myself stimulated to write in response to them. Yet somehow their
very excellence frightens me into inactivity. I know from conversations I have had, with people who regarded themselves as writing
for the first time, how easily we de-skill one another. I think this
is partly because our society gives us a view of the first rate and
original which is more to do with elitism than with encouraging
excellence. Few experiences are more telling than walking along a
railway platform past empty first class coaches so that you can get
into the second class or standard ones. Obviously our own background and temperament are sometimes part of the problem, but
it is also difficult if we consciously strive not to be hard, driving,
competitive, aggressive.

One of the difficulties and blocks is undoubtedly our fear of
showing other people what we write. I have been fascinated, on
the occasions when I have been privileged to encourage others to
write, to find that this fear is so widespread. A child puts her arm
around her work on the desk and says, 'No you cannot see my
drawing, not until I have finished.' The uncertain and hesitant
adult writes poetry and never shows anyone. So many people know
they have things they want to write and say but they feel they are
not good enough or that they cannot write in an acceptable way.
But we have to try.

When I look at a painting or sculpture, read a book, watch a
film, listen to some music, walk around London or some northern
market, talk with people, I am often attracted to join in. Somehow
we have to find ways of harnessing such encouragement, motivation, energy and creativity. We have to find how to channel our
own experiences into the words we shape from them.

Writing combines logical and lateral thinking. It should be like
a geological or archaeological expedition, an impressionist painting, a laser-made hologram: all at once! It should make our minds

and feelings surge so that we cannot put it down or get off to sleep. Yet at other times it should be able to slow us down to the point of silence. At best, and I think most importantly, it should create an experience of reality in itself. In other words, the writing becomes the experience and the experiences are caught in the process of writing. Writing should not only describe and tell how things are, it should show them.

Sometimes, I do feel strong and aware of what I want to write. The hesitancy goes. I know that I want to write in a clear and direct way. I want to take account of my own obsessiveness and the fragmented nature of my life. I want the way I write to fit and express the sense of what I write, so that there is a genuine consistency. I find I know when this happens. You get that feeling when you shake yourself, breathe out, empty your mind and the words come directly. Then I am satisfied with what I write.

It is important to realize that this statement about writing is not an admission of weakness which is to be discounted because it is untrue or inappropriate. It is, for me, an integral part of finding the way through.

I always remember a conversation with an Asian colleague and friend. Although he understands and speaks English both articulately and very intelligently he persists, in quite a wilful way, in retaining Asian thought patterns and structures of conversation. So he sometimes resolutely will not get to the point in our pointed and linear way. I remember saying to him once, 'I sometimes wish you were speaking a language other than English so that I would be able to stop pretending that I know what you are talking about.' In the same way we assume that we know what the shape a poem or novel or play should be, we have clear cut and quite restricted ideas of the formal shape that a painting, some music or a ballet should follow. And, in my limited experience, these assumptions are very strong when it comes to Western writing about spirituality and theology. Somehow I would like to find a style and way of writing that better fits with my experiences than the normal, formal, logical and linear approach. Of course I value these, indeed they are a part of me from which I cannot escape. But I would like also to write in a way which involves stories and narrative, lateral as well as logical thought, and in a way which can make a point other than in a straight line. I sense that such will be a perilous course to try to follow, and motorways are so much faster and quicker. But in this personal journey I hope I may travel with greater variety and inventiveness.

4 Blocks

Some external pressures keep blocking me. I know that I need to deal with them and address them before I can continue. One is the sheer level of information to which we are exposed. So much that we know about, through television, the press, books, videos, publicity, and all the rest is wholly outside our immediate lives. The media shows us many things which have power and influence over our lives but very often we have no way of responding or participating. Events, which are sometimes threatening and often dramatic, whirl around us. We sense the smallness of our planet but so much of it is well beyond our influence let alone our control. We may be able to see via TV and the press what is happening, at least in an edited version, at the touch of a switch, but we know deep down that we are out of touch with so much of what is happening. It seems to me that this experience has both good and bad effects upon us. We carry with us a greater amount of information about the world and, if we work at it, a greater appreciation and understanding of what is happening, and that is surely good. But the bad thing is that it can lead to a high degree of frustration because we can do so little about so much of it.

I have said that I want to write personally about things that I can influence. An image and experience that comes to me to illustrate this is to say that I want to write personally about things that happen whilst I am in the room. This phrase 'in the room' is a very vivid one to me. We live much of our lives in the relatively small rooms of our homes. We sometimes step through doorways and find ourselves in rooms which are strikingly different from the ones we are used to. We sometimes get involved with ideological world-views in the hope that we are stepping through doorways into spacious freedom only to find that we are in rooms which are curtained, shuttered and without exit. Decisions are taken, very often, by a small group of people meeting in a room. The power lies with those who are in the room. So often people who do not have power, or who are having adverse decisions made about them, are not invited to be in the room when that decision is made.

We have very limited opportunities for participation and joining in. What in fact many people do, as a means of coping, is to select and focus on issues which give them specific and limited opportunities to participate and join in. They join communities of interest as a means of finding friends, allies, contact and the possibility of limited achievement and fulfilment. I do not say this bitterly but it seems that there are very limited opportunities for most of us to join in. Government voting happens once every four or five years. For most people, rightly or wrongly, nothing else happens. Local government is virtually out of sight and hearing. In our neighbourhoods and communities we rarely meet, let alone work together on a common cause or for the common good. In the main we live individual and private lives and these are only extended by our decisions to include other people within our family, friends and acquaintances. The only other way in which we interact in our society is through these communities of interest. So we opt into certain sectors of society as we need them: housing, education, employment, health, welfare. We choose to belong to other communities of interest which focus for example on leisure or recreational interests, on consumerism and shopping, or on groups which share specific ideological concerns. We cluster, often with our own kinds of people, doing things we have in common. Above all, what we are free and able to do is in a large measure regulated by how much wealth and money we have. Our choices in our society are so often determined by that one factor.

So I want to write, above all else, about things which are happening to me at first hand. I am keen to understand more about what I can do. How I can be the sort of person that I want to be with all the decisions and choices I make and with all the limits and constraints of the situation and context within which I find myself. I want to write, not about those things about which I know at a distance or at second hand, but about those things, people, experiences and realities which I know directly and at first hand. So much that I see on the media, so much that crosses my desk at work, so much that swirls around us in the world is other than this. But I really would like to get at it and nail it and find it and see this brilliant, slippery, wonderful, terrible, now-here and now-gone thing that it is. I really would like to set it down.

5 Some stones to mark the way

I began, because of our children and through attempts to set things down in writing, to gather some stones with which to mark the way.

The image may seem a strange one for someone who lives his life in cities. It certainly is a very personal one and for me it is a very strong and striking image. I think of standing stones which are resonant with our history and prehistory. I think of sculptors who use stones and carve abstracted shapes in ways that I find so attractive and stimulating. I think of cairns of stones built to mark the highest point of a mountain or gathered in the cause of peace. I think of stones in a Zen Buddhist garden. I think also of the ways people use stones as milestones, for direction, in tracking, as landmarks, for boundaries. In addition to my personal liking for stones the idea of a traveller using stones to mark the way for those following is a common and evocative one.

As human beings we live for much of the time with complicated, unsystematized and even unformed attitudes and values. It is not always easy to detect the guidelines and trip wires that we are using to make decisions and form our actions. Even when we have a particular belief system we often live, in practice, with something of a rag bag of values, middle axioms, guidelines and rules of thumb. To say this is not to denigrate the seriousness or sincerity with which we hold our commitments or seek to make right decisions. It is rather to acknowledge that for most of us much of it is rather more piecemeal for more of the time than we realize or would care to admit.

Because I have found this to be true, not least in relation to the sharp and hard issues of living, I have tried to discover and hold on to a few simple and strong reference points. These are among those things which are important and precious to me. These are the stones that I want to set down so as to mark the way. In saying this I am in no way denying the complexity, compromise or lack of clarity which remains on so many issues. This is especially so when genuine conflict is involved. But, nevertheless, these stones do mark the way and act as markers which constantly provide direction. I want, at this point, to identify four of them.

The first that is important and precious to me is being life-affirming. This means caring above all else for all that creates, builds up and grows, as against that which destroys, breaks down and diminishes. I mean that this is the way I want to live my life.

It is not easy to say something that is so important so simply. It would be much easier to describe it in a more complicated and sophisticated way. It would be much easier to defend it with explanations and arguments. But the fact is that when I really examine what is important and precious to me and when I ask myself what is the first stone which I would put down to mark the way then this is certainly it. I come back to it through my experiences. It makes sense to me. It obsesses me. I come to it from endlessly different directions. I find it an idea, a value, a way of living which is attractive, satisfying, fulfilling. It is, in my better moments and my worst, how I want to be.

The second thing that is important and precious to me is to be at home in myself and in the world. By this I mean that I have some sense of satisfaction and fulfilment in my life even if, or especially if, there is much in my life that is to do with conflict and even more before which I am powerless to do anything. I need and want to feel at home in myself and in the world.

A long time ago I was part of a group relaxation and meditation exercise at a conference. The leader kept repeating the phrase, which he wanted us to use of our own bodies and of our true selves, 'and be at home there'. It is a phrase that has stuck with me over the years. It implies, I think, not that anything with which people feel at ease is all right but that, for any person to have a hope of being a full and mature person, there has to be a degree of consistency, relaxedness and cohesion. In speaking of all that creates, builds up and grows as that which I personally value, I am saying that it is within such, rather than that which destroys, breaks down and diminishes that I feel at home.

So let me give an ordinary and then a more serious example. Being at home and being part of what creates, builds up and grows means making the environment I live in as pleasing as I can. It includes tidying up, doing housework, putting up pictures, having cacti around. It includes being part of routines in the house, shopping, vacuuming, going to the bank, coping with machines breaking down, getting the family allowance. It also means more pleasurable and personal things like reading the papers, driving the car, making coffee, cooking, watching TV, sharing in our family life and in the school life of our children as well as the work life of my partner. Of course the people with whom I live sometimes interpret my activity as an obsession with tidiness and an almost neurotic search for order! Certainly I own up to wanting to complete things, and the Gestalt circle is deeply satisfying to me.

Being at home in what creates, builds up and affirms also applies on a much larger and more serious canvas. The Jewish scriptures include the challenge to choose life rather than death 'so that you and your descendents might live'. The fact of other people dying is constantly with us. It is present in news of famines, in disasters and in diseases, of which AIDS is the most recent. It also comes in more personal messages when people say to us, 'Have you heard that John has died?' or 'I have a bit of bad news, Shilpa sadly has died.' But although we shall all die, we must live with the confidence of those who have stood looking back at the reality of their own deaths and have shed their tears about it, because the challenge to be at home in the world is the challenge to embrace life. Sometimes in films there are battle scenes in which the hero presses forward with men falling on either side, till alone surviving (or with a few of the other highest paid actors!) he reaches safety. In our bleakest moments we experience our friends disappearing like that. They die, we find out, we make a suitable note in the address book and, at worst, it is as though they were never with us. So though we are constantly at risk to the terrible and the unknown I want to be at home in this world in such a way that I can be a part of that which chooses life rather than death. I understand that this vision and hope is as fragile as my body and can be easily crushed by pain and suffering, power and violence. But I choose this way. I may not be able to choose it completely or perfectly, but I can choose it as consciously, fully and frequently as I can.

The third stone is to do with pursuing truth. It is not just a matter of trying to tell the truth or even of trying to find out what is true in a particular situation, hard as both these are. It is that, in some deep way, that I certainly do not fully understand, I think reality, existence and being are bound up together with truth. Putting it very crudely, they are of the same stuff and you cannot prise them apart. Only when we care deeply about the truth and struggle to find it can we hope to engage our planet and our human existence on authentic terms.

Truth is like running across the countryside. You have to go beyond the pain barrier and you come over the hill to the descent, before the long hard road through the council housing estate and the dogs snapping at you. Before that, I remember, there was a sense of exhilaration as you dug into your reserves of energy, as you put aside tiredness and headed for home.

I think truth has that directness, freshness, clarity and simplicity. I wish I could hold such truth in my hands like a beautiful piece of slate. It makes me want to hold it up to the light to examine it, knowing that it is both dense and ephemeral. So I care more about truth and wisdom than I do about information. There are such utter and appalling untruths on sale in every market place, government, arms exhibition. The media is all too often full of the chatter of violent lies. Our marvellous computer systems are too often used for disinformation and control. And, of course, there is the sheer volume and weight of information which overwhelms us: on TV, in libraries, encyclopaedias, and book shops. Somehow truth is to do with a deep desire to complete the circle and see the Gestalt whole. Truth and wisdom have a pattern, like the DNA code, a snow flake, the galaxies. Some people believe that there is no pattern and that the search for one is illusory and self-deceiving. They think that, quite literally, it does not make sense. I find that truth and wisdom are very important to me in their many-faceted, complex and diverse ways. So we have to set them down as we are able.

The fourth stone to mark the way and introduce those things which are especially important and precious to me is to do with the struggle for justice and peace. It would be possible to try to be life-affirming, to seek to be at home in yourself, to pursue truth and to do it without really coming up against the reality and need of most people's lives. It would be possible to ignore our common humanity and the compassion which is motivated by our interdependence.

There are three quite hard comments which I carry with me as I write this. The first is the charge that all this is so much dilettante luxury compared with the crying needs of the world's starving: I hear this and in one sense I have no answer to it. The second is that in some ways my own life is both particular and protected. It is certainly true that by being a minister of religion within the Methodist Church I follow a vocation which, though in certain ways demanding, excuses me from some of life's toughness and bloodiness. But, in any case, I am conscious of how easy it is to leave important things out because they do not fit comfortably within our own views. The third is that, as so many other people have found, most of us who want to get at things in a new and fresh way end up, for example in a book, which looks suspiciously like all that has gone before.

I mention these now because I am thinking of people who have said these three things to me. They are criticisms which rightly ask if my life itself, let alone this writing, has in fact anything to do with the major issues of our society and world which, in a phrase, are all to do with justice, peace and the integrity of creation.

I cannot see that we can speak of being life-affirming, at home in ourselves, and truth, without at the same time acknowledging through our dependence on other people and our common humanity that the struggle and search for justice and peace are vitally important.

This commitment to justice, peace and the integrity of creation takes many forms around the world. But in all cases it enables people and groups to become involved in social and political issues. In some situations and for some people the issues of justice and peace cannot be avoided because it affects their very survival. If people are hungry and starving, if people have their most fundamental human rights denied them, if national minorities or ethnic groups are constantly disadvantaged and treated as inferior and third-rate citizens or as non-citizens, or if people's lives are totally disrupted and at risk because of war, then there is no way that the issues of justice and peace can be avoided. They cannot be separated from a person's own survival and fulfilment. But in our society many people are able to keep their private and personal lives distinct from what is happening socially and politically. People do this by keeping different parts of their lives and experiences apart and compartmentalized. So, for example, a person who works in the inner city may see the problems of the inner city wholly differently when they are at home in their suburban and comfortable life style. But for those who are relatively poor, for those groups which are disadvantaged, and for any who are willing to take sides in this struggle about justice and peace these political issues become part of personal living. The recognition of our common humanity and the concern that people are treated fairly and even-handedly, in both personal and structural terms, means engaging with others in this struggle. We act for justice and peace as though the injustices and conflict were happening to us.

Because we all join in, as I have said, part way through, I decided to start very firmly with what is important and precious to me. I began with our children and my writing. I have recognized some blocks. I have used the image of setting down stones to mark the way as a means of focussing on what is important and precious to me. I have expressed them without arguing why they matter to me so much, let alone why, or on what basis, they might or should matter to other people. I have simply and, I hope, straightforwardly come out with it and said that in my experience these four things are really important and precious to me.

They are:
– being life-affirming and caring above all else for that which creates, builds up and grows, as against that which destroys, breaks down and diminishes;
– seeking to be at home both in myself and in the world;
– pursuing truth and authenticity;
– struggling for justice, peace and the integrity of creation on the basis of our common and interdependent humanity.

6 Ways forward

Now the fact is that if all I wanted to do was to show what is important and precious to me in my life I could stop at this point. It would be, as I have said, expressed for our children and expressed quite rightly in a very personal way. I have discovered, in all my many attempts to set down what is important and precious to me, that I care about much more than simply showing and describing this way of living. I know that I want to do several things more.

But I have found that in attempting to do them I get myself into a mess or find myself entangled in several processes that I do not really understand. I say entangled, but they feel like overlapping and demanding influences. I find myself both entwined and blocked by them. I am not going to be side-tracked, yet again, by trying to grasp what it is precisely that confuses and blocks me.

I want to do three things.

I want to show as well as I am able the personal experiences and raw materials of my life which are the situation and context within which I come to what is important and precious to me.

I want also to describe, in several interlocking ways, how these life-values fit into my faith as a Christian. In other words having begun from what is actually happening to me in my life and having included within that, of course, my Christian faith, I want to go on to a further step of Christian critical reflection.

I am now going to look at these in some detail in Parts One and Two. Then in Part Three I will try to see, with all the difficulties, how it works in practice.

PART ONE

Personal Experiences and Raw Materials

1 Making the list

I am starting directly from my own experience. This is for me the
right way forward because, regardless of what sense I make of the
world around me, I have to get on with living my life. I think of
these and call these, rather pragmatically, the raw materials of my
personal life. Obviously they are very personal. Indeed there is
something quite fiercely personal in what I include and exclude.
But the most striking thing about them for me is that these experiences, issues, ideas, actions are ones to which I return over and
over again. I come back to them as being important and precious
regardless of what I make of other people's values and actions. On
one level they are very ordinary. As someone said when I tried to
share them, 'My waste paper basket is full of such rubbish.' Quite!
But in another sense they are private and personal in a way that
suggests that all of us have or need to have our own versions of this
list of personal raw materials.

For me the words 'raw materials' have become quite powerful.
They carry the idea of certain things that are basic. Raw materials
are in common use, they are therefore widely available, and they
are to be used for some purpose. Moreover, there is the suggestion,
within the idea, that raw materials can and will be used in different
proportions and different mixtures at various times and according
to particular needs and conditions. So, as I say, the idea is many-
layered and quite richly evocative.

2 Doorways into pluralism

Of all the things that happen to me in my life few are clearer or
more influential than the experience of stepping through a doorway into a room. Often someone opens the door from the inside
and invites you in. Or again you are taken along by someone and
they open the door for you. It has happened to me so many times,
you step through a doorway into a room and it is as though you
have entered another world. It looks different, sounds and smells
different, people have different customs, activities and languages.

Let me open a few doors by way of example.

In secular terms I think of what living in East London has
meant for us as a family. Living here, going to church here, working here, going to school locally, all has meant that secular culture
has become our normal way of seeing the world. Of course we see
good and bad within it. It is strange that whilst we are at home
there it is in fact unrelentingly and effortlessly not religious. You
see it in the smiling but puzzled faces of people at a church wed-
ding, you know it in the lives of your own children and those of
your friends. Part of it is to do with science and technology. The
sheer level and extent of inventiveness and rapid change is breathtaking. It comes at us through the machines we try to buy in the
shops in order to keep up. Within this hardware we sometimes
find ourselves so far behind that it is as though we are using candle-
light instead of fibre optics and lasers. And behind all this there is
a level of research into what our universe is actually like and how
it works, which for most people I suspect barely surfaces in any
way that we can grasp, let alone systematize. So we carry around
with us some technical machinery and the sense that astonishingly
brilliant things are happening but we also have the sense of our
own ignorance. All this is part of our secular and scientific experience and it is a strange mixture with its instant and obvious pay-
offs, with its deep criticism of past theories, and yet with its
difficulties in communicating its most important findings.

Another example is in going to an art gallery. Now of course
they come in all shapes and sizes. But take an exhibition of very
modern art, which I enjoy looking at. Sometimes what is shown is
quite shockingly and extraordinarily different. Negatively it makes

you ask if what is on show is worth anything. Positively it excites, challenges, angers, pleases. There is the ambience of the particular place itself. It has hidden assumptions about the type of art which will be displayed, the cost of food which is on sale, the selection of people who go there. So you look round and you know that you are partly influenced by what you know, by names you recognize, by the whole concept of what is famous or, the even more slippery one, of what is commercial. A child looks round and makes the complaint that some of the art is rubbish. He shouts out that the emperor really is without clothes. At times, compared with the needs of the world I have left behind, the exhibits seem trivial and wasteful. At other times their energy, inventiveness, creativity, daring, make my mind and emotions wide open.

Over the last decade or so I have gone to quite a number of services of Christian worship in the black Pentecostal type of church. Whenever I do this I find I have to alter my way of responding. Some of it I find quite difficult. I have to let go of my individualistic approach and I have to try to suspend my critical and analytical method which depends so much on words and concepts. Putting it positively, I have to respond more emotionally, more physically, more collectively. If I am willing to do this and to join in on the terms of the worship, I find there an energy which is very warm, positive and enriching. It is of course, at times, extremely intense. I remember once in the middle of a service, with people singing, being filled with the Spirit, laid down in the aisles, and lining up to be blessed, two small children. They were girls of perhaps three years of age. They were standing on the pew seat dancing and singing. Each one had a tambourine of the sort without a skin but with bells. They were so beautiful. Suddenly, in a moment of escape from the sheer intensity of what was happening around me, I felt to pull back out away from it all, and it seemed as though, ridiculously, these two tiny children were controlling all that was happening.

And, of course, there are very many other faith systems. To speak of world faiths used to mean referring to other places and other countries. But now Europe, and East London within it, has become a meeting place for world faiths. Some people are thrilled and excited by this. Others are frightened and appalled. It is strange that a society which, in one sense, is rightly described as secular, should also be a meeting place for such a diversity of beliefs. So, to say that in East London between our peoples, in our schools, in our communities we have regular contact between Christians, Jews, Muslims, Hindus, Sikhs, Buddhists, Marxists, Humanists, and people giving allegiance to many smaller groupings, is to say no more than the truth. This is how it is. They represent and present world faiths whose identity, in our context at least, is partly shaped by the fact that they are one faith amongst many. Through friends and through groups committed to interfaith dialogue I have been able to know more than the surface of some other faiths. We have seen, as happens within our own faith, what lies beneath the surface of personal discipline and public ritual. For some people the phenomena of religion really do provide some things which are important and precious. Others find the daily traditions and customs within their family life liberating. But behind both I have often found people of devotion and loyalty, people who have in valuing their own faith been willing to be open and sensitive to other people.

I was brought up never to go into pubs. I remember one of my first visits. We were in a small dark room, noisy with happiness and activity, after walking along some fairly poor streets in a northern city. I looked at the bar with the variety of bottles and machines to dispense them and at the people sitting around the small tables. I saw the younger people energetically playing pool. The atmosphere was relaxed. For most of the people there I would think that this was their regular. For the small group I was with, it was ours, for the evening. I felt, in spite of being with people I knew well and was very fond of, out of place, self-conscious, somewhat guilty. But as the evening went on, and after a few glasses of lemonade and lime, I began to understand something of what was happening.

We go through a different sort of doorway when we encounter foreign languages. When I went to my first large public event in South Wales I was invited to introduce the first hymn at the combined service. 'It is all ready for you in the pulpit' said the minister from Heol Fawr. When the time came I went up into the pulpit, looked out rather nervously over the hundreds of people, smiled, looked down at the hymn book and found, too late, that it was in Welsh. When my wife was doing her thesis at college it involved her in visiting Muslim families and so sometimes I was taken along to ease the social process. Once we went to my home town and whilst my wife did her work talking with the women I was taken into a house with the men. There I found myself, within a short distance of where I was born, listening to a heated conversation about the Koran and the Bible, in Urdu, with me turning towards one speaker after another, and, of course, without understanding a word. A longer and less personal experience was sitting for several hours at a turban ceremony for a Sikh colleague. After a time, in someone else's language, you almost begin to feel you should or do understand.

Sometimes the doorways are not physical. Not far from where we live, near to the road, there is a wide expanse of fields. On it there meets, what I assume to be, for I have never gone and asked, a model aeroplane club. Cars park to watch. Men and children fly and adjust their remote-controlled planes. You can hear them droning if you walk along 'the flats'. They meet in an area where there are also football matches, cricket matches, volley ball, par-ascending, running, horse riding, and at certain times of year a fair ground and a circus. I mention these because, whatever the formal arrangements may or may not be, the model flying club appears to meet as though it were under its own roof, or at least, its own sky.

I think, to give a final few examples, of young black Britons I have met who are trying to find a way of being British which is also faithful to their roots and identity in Africa or the Caribbean. I think especially, through my wife's work over the years, of young Asian women living between two cultures and wanting both to be a modern young woman and a 'good' Hindu, Muslim or Sikh daughter. I think of Rastafarians choosing sometimes to live a separatist culture. I think of some feminists and feminist groups who are seeking to find ways of living, deciding, organizing which are consistent with their understanding of themselves. I think of times when I have been in Wales, perhaps at some cultural event which ends with the national anthem of Wales, and I have felt something of the power and energy and attractiveness of belonging to a small nation: and yet I see how hard it is for such a nation to keep and develop what is essential to its Welshness. I could go on. I am not saying that everyone traffics between all these groups, nor am I denying the antipathy or, at times, the conflicts between them. I am saying simply that their existence, vitality, richness, diversity is to be valued. Not least in the face of all that presses us towards an individualistic, privatized, consumer-orientated, mono-chrome society.

These sort of experiences could be repeated over and over again. What I am saying is that in our society it is possible, and for many people entirely normal, to step through doorways into rooms which can be described, not over dramatically, as other worlds. Indeed I want to press the point and suggest that this is a very necessary perception. I do not believe that we can begin to under-stand what our life is all about until we recognize that it is made up of many world-views, languages, cultures and groups. In one sense of course this is self-evident. But in fact many people live as though there were only one world-view or that of all the world-views the only one that has any value and merit is their own.

In fact there are many, many worlds and languages. These in-clude: computers, maths, music, Sanskrit, ice hockey, braille, sign language, cooking, doing crafts, studying anthropology, learning Greek or Anglo-Saxon, watching a film in a foreign language, going to the theatre, dancing to pop music, trooping the colour, going to an indoor athletics meeting, visiting a car racing circuit, reading a particular academic discipline, and so on.

You have, when you enter new worlds, to give yourself time to settle in, become attuned, get in the right language, hear what is being offered and presented, and be sensitive to what is intended. It matters a great deal that when we are talking to one another we make certain that we are in the same world-view and that we get into the appropriate and agreed language. You have to be in the right mode, in the mood, in gear, in the right world.

3 Our ordinary lives

Sometimes when I go to a city or a town for the first time I enjoy walking around it at quite a fast pace. I am fascinated by the view I get at street level. I try to understand what it all signifies. It is something I do as I walk through the streets of the borough where we live. Always there are clues, signs, warnings, experiences. I want to begin describing the raw materials of my life at the equivalent of street level. I want, if I can, to get at the ordinary things I take for granted and which, in fact, make up a great deal of my life.

Before doing that I want to recognize just how much I take for granted, at least in terms of having food, shelter, clothing, security. I know a little about how many people there are in our world who have none of these. It was a Latin American writer who made the hurtful and true comment that people do theology after they have eaten. This is a way of saying that there is a fundamental and almost unbridgable gap between those of us who have more than enough to live by and all those who will die tomorrow from hunger. The thing that is unbearable, or would be if we allowed the facts to confront us, is that such hunger could be avoided. The world is more than able to feed all its people. Only the political will is lacking.

But though this is true and important to me it is not directly within my life. That is to say I am able, rightly or wrongly, to distance myself from it. This, to put it the other way round, is not what is happening to me in the ordinary experiences of my daily life. One of the things that I am conscious of is just how important it is, wherever we are and in whatever state we find ourselves, to try to live within that reality. A colleague of mine has used the phrase 'the future is always somewhere else' to describe people's longing to move from East London to a more prosperous location. In a way the idea and image goes even deeper than that. Even when we are in one place there are constant temptations to escape. We are tempted to deny the power we actually have or the responsibility we have. We are encouraged to reach after possessions we do not have and cannot afford. We are challenged to embrace political and ideological programmes which are remote from our real lives. Somehow we have to live in the present here.

So what happens? We sleep, make love, eat, work, go to the toilet, drink coffee, meet people. Sometimes we are hurt or angered or pleased by people. We watch TV, do housework, go to the dentist, are ill, travel by underground, catch buses or trains to see family or go on holiday, we walk across estates, visit friends, go to church. We shop, spend money and worry about saving money, rest, learn to use gadgets, see beautiful things, draw, try to cope with the news on TV, worry about the people we love. We plan, go to banks, cope with minor ailments, water the plants, change the beds, do the cooking. This is both an inadequate and yet necessary way of describing the raw material of my life. It really matters to see it and grasp it in its ordinariness.

I believe this is so because any sense or meaning that we have is constructed from such raw materials. We have to make up our own sense in order to have a view of ourselves and our own identity and health. We have to make sense in order to have values with which to relate to other people. I have tried, many times, to make all this more concrete, and to flesh out the raw materials through recounting moments, conversations and stories which enhance my living. But in listing the very ordinary things of living I am emphasizing that they are in themselves part of the sense which offers a way through.

Let me focus on a few of these ordinary things.

All of us look back to our childhood. We remember leaving home. We remember, perhaps, going back home and all that that experience revealed about our childhood. We have, through such experiences, some idea of what it means to be at home and feel at home in ourselves. And, through our contact with people who have migrated and settled in our country, we have some grasp of the problems and opportunities which come with such movement. We know the antagonism which comes when people are treated as strangers, foreigners and aliens. In looking back we see something of the fabric of our most ordinary lives.

There are some people who have good memories and some who do not. There are some people I know who can recall details from the very early days of their childhood. I cannot. When I look back therefore I find myself with general memories and impressions. On the whole I am quite satisfied with them but occasionally, when I am listening to someone whose recall is much more extensive, I do feel rather envious of their skill.

In a way our need to look back and be sure about our roots is, as I said earlier, all to do with our very specific location. Certainly I found that it was only when I went back to my home area as an adult, because of my work, that I began to understand its strengths and peculiarities. I know people whose childhood has been so traumatic and damaging that they have never become free of it. I know others whose uncertainty and confusion about their own identity stems from those early days. I know other people who in going back and rediscovering their roots, in parents, or a place, or even another country, have found new dignity and confidence.

When I was at home I would say my experiences were, with exceptions, generally and genuinely happy. I have a good feeling about all that happened within our small family. What I realize now, and I do not know how true it is for everyone, is that I had little consciousness or awareness of what was happening to me. I did not, at that time, know much of other world-views. I lived happily and securely, for the most part, within a family, school, church and local neighbourhood which were very much of a piece. It was only really in leaving home that I began to see what it had all been about.

I sometimes wonder looking back how we can unravel and detect those influences which really make us what we are. I do not mean in the obvious psychological sense but rather how we evaluate and understand the relative weight and effect of all that guides and shapes us.

Another example is that of sleeping and dreaming. It is odd and disconcerting that this takes up, for many people, almost a third of their lives, and yet we have little memory or knowledge of it. I certainly enjoy sleeping but hardly ever remember dreams. I understand that it is possible to learn to remember and, of course, even learn to interpret and understand them. But I have not, as yet, learnt the skill.

I recall though, when our children were about six, our son coming downstairs one morning and telling us that he had had a most vivid dream. There was nothing unusual in this because for a time both children enjoyed telling their nightly adventures. But this dream was strangely direct. He said that in it an elderly Hindu friend of ours had appeared and given him some words. These words the man said, described human life. The words were 'joy and struggle'. It was all very odd. Yet the words have stayed with me as a gift, clear, brief and sharp edged.

I have learnt that the boundary between being asleep and being awake is less clear than I used to believe. I say this because I have woken from sleep or been asleep and asked myself whether or not what I was hearing and seeing was a dream or waking. Sometimes it has been pleasant and I have continued sleeping or gone back to sleep. At other times it has been frightening and certainly once I

remember falling out of bed as I reached towards the fearsome
person who stood between the bed and the door.

I give the two examples from our children and myself so as to
acknowledge that I recognize there is much within myself about
which I know almost nothing. Although I regret this, and although
I wish it were otherwise, in fact I live as though it were not
important.

So let me move to a final and rather different example of
ordinariness. We all have to learn to deal with the experience of
losing and winning. It may be an exam, a race, a driving test, a
job, a partner, or an election. But there is a crucial difference between losing occasionally and getting into the position or finding
yourself in the position where constant daily defeats erode and
corrode your self-confidence and human dignity. There can be too
many defeats; too many losses; too little opportunity for manoeuvre, choice or freedom. At such times, and under such stress,
we tend not only to make wrong choices and be unhappy, we also
tend to become ill. Our dis-ease is often tied in with our inability
to resist or reverse all that denies and diminishes us as people.
The same I believe is true of groups. This is why minorities are so
vulnerable in every country and in every situation. It is also why
those who belong to 'cognitive minorities' have to be wide awake
to their own propensity to pathological behaviour and attitudes.
Winning also has its own particular rewards and dangers.

It is a little odd to try to emphasize the ordinariness of something! I do so for several reasons. First, this is the world I in fact
inhabit. Second, the further I am away from subsistence and starvation the easier it is to ignore and even deny the ordinary facts of
my life. Thirdly, in trying to get at what is important and precious
to me, it is vital that I hold up to the light those things which,
though ordinary, in fact fill my days. Otherwise I am neither going
to get any sense of proportion in how I live nor am I going to learn
to value what is commonplace. As in so much of what I am saying,
my own examples are simply that. They are not the whole story
for me. They are intended to be illustrations, which other people
can use, or replace, to get hold of the ordinariness of their own
lives.

There is a deep and creative sense in which things are what they
are. Their reality, their density, their sheer otherness over against

me, their givenness are all part of that world of humanity that we earthlings inhabit. I only need to say this, because so much thought and practice denies it, or at least, pulls us away from it. This is it! And our capacity to encounter and make sense of 'all this' world of ordinariness is, on one crucial level at least, vital to our survival and fulfilment as human beings. In spite of every threat and every fluid relativity, our ordinary lives have a breathtaking solidness about them.

4 People

Within this ordinariness, certain things stand out very clearly. Above all there is the importance of people. Now, as I have found myself saying several times, in one sense no one needs to draw anyone else's attention to the importance of people. It is, to say the least, not easy to avoid them. But extraordinarily, whilst our common humanity is probably the most obvious and certain fact of our human existence, so much of human history and experience is spent in denying that reality. To say that all people are of value and worth and to say that our identity is only fully realized through our interdependence and within the community of humankind is to make a claim which flies in the face of human history.

Nonetheless, in East London I find, not only that there are a lot of people around, not only that they are very different from each other, but that they are important to me. I know people who find walking along busy crowded streets a joyful and enlightening experience. They find in the eyes and faces of strangers an affirmation of a common humanity which is formed, for them, within countless more personal and intimate conversations. Certainly people are a major part of the story of what it means to be human. There are times when the harshness and cruelty people show to each other is unbearable. Sometimes we hear too much. There is too much unclenched anger, too many beaten women, too much crime, too many children who have lost the knack of trusting, too many old people whose cultures have become a corpse of reactionary tradition. Yet, also, people feed us. We find strength in our families, friends, neighbours, at school, at work, with the people we have to meet regularly, within church groups, even with people who seek to hurt us and do us harm. Often we see families coming apart and sometimes we know enough pressure and tiredness in our family to begin to hurt and reject one another. We survive, but sometimes only with great effort. At times there is sheer grind, hard work, conflict and anger. At other times there are marvellous moments. There are times for us as a family and with friends, around the meal table or in worship or whilst watching TV, when the blessing of our common humanity is apparent.

Let me try to give four examples and pictures of what I mean.

If you go to the Himalayas, or even to the English Lake District, the Scottish Highlands or Snowdonia in Wales, there is a sense of givenness. Obviously much is happening to mountains, both ecologically and, in Britain, because of people. In a way I experience a city like London, and to some extent British society, like a mountain. You constantly see them changing, with new roads, buildings, shops, markets, galleries, housing, tourist attractions. But the overriding sense is one of continuity. It is so big that all you can do is join in on its terms. I think in a very real sense that many of us in Britain live in relation to other people and society like this. The mountain is there and we are on it, a part of it, can alter it marginally, but mostly we experience it as something which is given to us, for good and ill.

It is not surprising, to come to my second example, that our society is an individualistic and private one. There are so few places where most people have the opportunity to meet or make decisions about their lives. This is true, generally, of government, work, communities, just to give some obvious situations. We live, not so much within neighbourhood communities, but, as I said earlier, within our self-selected communities of interest. There are the issues and sectors of society with which we are involved. We engage aspects of society at specific times and at specific need points in our lives. But on the whole, for most of us most of the time, we are private individuals, with our small families and any extension to that family which we choose to develop. Sometimes, when I watch TV programmes about specific community projects in the developing 'third world', I am really surprised to find that those projects are being undertaken by a whole community about the needs of a whole community. In one sense it is right to say this has been impossible within British society for generations. It does not even happen within villages. But in a world in which people are to be valued and in which our common humanity is our most striking reality we find ourselves in a society which pulls and keeps us apart.

My third picture is an extreme one. In July 1985 there was a TV event called 'Live Aid'. It sought to raise money for the famine victims of Africa and the Sahel. It was, at one and the same time, an event for others and an event of global significance in itself. Usually world systems freeze us all into our political divisions and warring ideologies. Usually we are so overcome by the threats and warmongering of rivals that we do little to discover what can be done when we act together. On that day the slogan 'feed the world' was used with all the paraphernalia of the rock music industry and all the hype of TV. Nonetheless, it presented not only an opportunity to give money to help people but an opportunity to view the world in a truly global way. The event pushed the millions who watched nearer towards a shared future. It brought before us, as the photographs of the earth from space had done years before, an image of such clarity, simplicity and radicalness that we were challenged by it. This time it was in the faces and tiny hands of dying African children.

My last example is ordinary in the sense that some version of it can happen to me whenever I choose to go from our house and walk within a half mile radius of it. Some time ago I found the street more full with cars than usual and wondered what was happening. As I went past the church round the corner of our street I could see that a black Pentecostal church was holding a convention there. I went on to the Greek Cypriot breadshop and resisted buying the superb gateaux but bought fresh bread, green olives, taramasalata, and some salami meat. I then went into the Asian sweet shop and got some chocolate burfi. On the way home, having crossed the road on both occasions when someone actually stopped for me on the zebra crossing, I noticed a man. He was a tramp, vagrant, street person. I recognized him by sight. He was using his walking stick to open out on the pavement a large piece of plastic sheeting which, I assume, had blown there. He was no doubt going to use it for shelter.

Even in these four limited pictures it is possible to see how people are at once a challenge, threat and encouragement to us.

The question is how we can be human, earthlings, people, communities. How can we affirm both our own identity and the fact of our interdependence within community?

Before giving two straightforward answers, let me recall a few more people. I had been involved for years, in a modest way, in the anti-apartheid movement. I got involved in some mild non-violent action. We were, on a hot sunny day, going to wash peoples' feet as they went into Christian worship from the conference they were attending. It was slightly presumptuous but we felt it was a sincere attempt to make the point. I put off the feet washing as long as I could for, after all, who really wants to wash the feet of strangers? Then my turn came and as I washed this man's white feet and as he expressed his gratitude for the service on such a hot sight-seeing day I asked him, before explaining the purpose of our demonstration, where he came from. 'South Africa', he said.

I recall also a different experience. Quite unexpectedly I was able to visit a relative a few days before, in fact, he died. He asked me to help him out of bed which I did. And then, with his wonderful sense of dry humour, he remarked, as he began coughing fiercely, 'Give me a bang on the back. Perhaps you'll knock it out of me.'

More recently a local person I know who is out of work, quite poor and in fairly bad health, met with some church people who had come to look round the inner city. He was one of a group who, after a service and lunch, took part in a walk-about. He found it difficult to get the surbanites to listen to him, even though he was one of the few people present who was born and bred in the place and knew it from well before the war. As he talked with me about how rejected he felt by people who would not listen to him he said, 'It's not just what you say is it, it's the love you show to people that matters.' I could go on describing more of the people I have known, all their energy, pride, grief, joy, resilience. But two things stand out.

Somehow the experience of people enables us to stand in other people's shoes. I recall years ago a TV programme about an educational psychologist. One of the experiments showed a model of a village with trees and mountains. A person stood on one of the four sides and was asked to describe, without moving, what it was like from one of the other sides. Apparently children only learn to do this after a certain age. What is tragically true is that some people never learn to stand in other people's shoes and remain incapable of such empathy or sympathy. I cannot see how we can survive let alone be fulfilled without acquiring this facility and insight.

In the same way I believe we have to learn to listen to other people. We have to strive to listen to all that people are saying to us about their lives and worlds. Of course at times it is impossible. At times we cannot bear it. But, as we affirm our common humanity and see something of what we are as people, this seems to me to be a crucial way through to mutual understanding and full recognition of each other's humanity.

5 Personal and political

This humanity is both personal and political. I have found it necessary, in order to get at the raw materials of my life, to have some framework and some sense of direction. It focusses on these two factors: the personal and the political.

I have some sense of a personal quest. That is to say my life, and all that happens to me, feels more like being on a journey or a pilgrimage than being entrenched in a secure building or rooted within one place. I remember, when I used to move house quite frequently, the feeling that home was where I managed to get all my books out on the shelves. My family teased me for years about my annual sorting out and packing which was not to do with spring cleaning but with the timing of moves within my particular work. But I do not think the sense of quest only comes from those early experiences. I think it also comes from a way of viewing and living in the world. It really does feel as though so much is on the move and changing that the only way to live is to be on a journey yourself.

I have built upon this simple idea because, whilst the Way of Jesus is an old description of the Christian way, it has become so clear to me that our society is made up of many ways. In a sense my visions of what I and the world might be like, my discovery of key end-words which for me sum up and describe what that world might be like, my identification of certain middle axioms as sayings which actually help me to find a way through decision making, have all been within this sense of being part of a quest. I know some of the ancient and even antique associations of the word but I think it has about it a certain individuality and clarity which I find attractive.

Alongside and overlapping this personal quest there is my involvement in and concern for the political issues of humanity and society. I sometimes have tried to sort out the relation between these two. There is the personal and interpersonal as against the socio-political, there is the spirituality of the first as against the politics of the second, there is the concern for contemplation as against the stance of resistance. But over the years I have come to see that these twins of spirituality and politics are not only overlapping realities but are in a relation of energy and dynamism. I have found a great part of my working life, especially in the years in East London, taken with the issues of humanity and society. It is no mere chance that experience here has led me into commitment and participation with a local church that has a lively community work programme in an inner city area. Nor again that my own more specialist work on issues of racial justice should be a means to my own political conscientization. I feel often that because of this I have been dragged almost reluctantly from the relative security and long familiarity with my personal quest into a harder and sharper-edged world. There the issues of humanity and society constantly make demands which go far beyond our energy, power or resources.

In practice the church in Britain has resisted political involvement except in so far as the church supports the monarchy, the establishment or the *status quo*. Indeed some people, with great political acumen, seek to limit the Christian faith and the Christian church to being a private and personal matter. This must be resisted, not because the church or priests especially want to 'meddle in politics', but because there is truly no part of human life which lies outside the domain of God's Kingdom or outside the Christian's responsibility.

The realization that my personal quest and the political issues of humanity and society fit together has been quite liberating. It has forced me to stop trying to fit experiences within one or other of these two categories and to see the spiritual or political dimension within each. I have come to understand, and this is a major step against the mainstream of Western thought and practice, that it does not make sense to separate religion from the rest of life; to separate the individual from the collective; or to view political understanding as other than an integral vein or perspective within the whole.

Of all the issues which are important within the personal and political, four stand out: religion, political power, money and sex. They are not only the themes of block-buster novels or the headlines of the tabloids, they are the raw material of everyone's life.

6 Belonging to the Christian church

As a Christian I know from my daily experience that much as being a Christian matters to me it is just one of the many options which the world offers. What is, in some ways, harder to bear is that within the Christian family, which can be variously described, are widely different beliefs and practices. So the first important thing to say is that it is wisest to distrust statements which claim too much consensus.

My way of being a Christian makes me feel rather edgy. By this I mean both that I feel somewhat on the edge (and against the tide) of what I believe and practice and that I experience a certain unease and friction as I strive to be at home in my faith.

Once upon a time, so the story goes, everyone believed in God. Everyone, well all right-thinking Westerners, shared the same view of the world: a sort of one up, one down, and you at the centre of life. It was a view which encompassed mythology, history and politics, to name a few. It was a world-view, so it is said, which made Britain what it is today: post-colonial, capitalist, post-Christian, an island off Europe. The fact that our nations now include a relatively small percentage of people who have come from different parts of the world, and that we have made the most enormous fuss and caused a great deal of real hurt and bitterness only goes to show how reluctant we are to let go of one way of seeing.

Some years ago I was at an inter-faith dialogue conference in West Germany. We talked and lived together as Jews, Christians and Muslims. The greatest impact was made upon me by the

British Jews because I learned from them that my experience was so like theirs. They experienced Britain as a Christian country within which they felt a minority. I experienced Britain as a secular country within which those of us who are Christians are in a minority. It was an important experience which was only strengthened as I stood in the Jewish graveyard, in the grounds, and saw that all the dates of the graves stopped before the inhabitants of the village were taken to the Nazi camps.

This fact of belonging to what has been called a cognitive minority seems to me enormously important. As far as religious belief is concerned most of Western Europe is, in practice, non-theistic. Those of us who hold on to any religious beliefs are seen by others to be hanging on to a world-view which sails dangerously close to the flat earth theory or the Pendle witches. If our cultures are sensate – that is 'empirical, this-worldly, secular, humanistic, pragmatic, ultilitarian' – then those who belong to a cognitive minority have a view of the world that is significantly different. Given that knowledge in this sense always refers to what is taken to be or believed as knowledge, such a minority is formed around deviant knowledge. So it is not surprising that I feel somewhat edgy.

For me being a Christian has meant reading, studying and using the Gospels of Jesus. During the last thirty years I have spent several hours each week studying them and several hours each week teaching them. Some people can turn the whole Jewish Bible or the whole Christian New Testament into their own private language. That is to say they work at it in such a way that it becomes part of their current, contemporary life and is wholly relevant to them. I have found that it takes all my limited skill and energy to do this with the four Gospels. I see them as within the Christian world-view and yet occupying the present. For all their complexity, for all the critical questions which have to be faced, they are accessible to me and offer a way of living which I believe is recognizably one way. Certainly there are four overlapping pictures. Certainly, as with the rest of the scriptures, the Gospels need understanding in their time and place. But they also provide much sense, challenge, stimulation and evocativeness. Of course there are many books that can be taken as a sacred text and as a starting point for wisdom, devotion and creative study. I have found these endlessly fascinating. I retain my obsession with them.

Christians come to God through Jesus. So I find it reasonably easy to grasp something of the God to whom Jesus points. I can sketch a little of the territory of God's Kingdom. I know this Kingdom is elusive, now here, now there. I know it is all to do with justice and righteousness, love and that peace which is of the shalom of God. I know from Jesus' teachings and actions that we are more likely to stumble across or be seized by God's Kingdom when we are with people, involved in healing, resisting evil, or passionate about righteousness and justice than if we are trying to, as it were, unravel God's DNA code.

But for me the radical critics are right when they say that a view of God outside our world and our human understanding is both self-contradictory and superstitious. It is difficult to say this properly. In one sense to say it is to say no more than that humans can only understand within human limits, which though true is tautologous. But in denying that God, as known to us through Jesus, is beyond us we are asserting our freedom and independence from what has been called 'a God of the gaps' and what might be termed 'a truly alien God' or a 'God who is so unknowable as to be unimportant'. I am not going to expand on this unbelief. What I want rather to point to is that in my experience with the Gospels of Jesus I find myself at odds with some of what has always been presumed to go with it.

Pressing on this point is rather like pressing on the nerve when you have toothache. For most of the time the Christian church does not approach the question of God head on any more, if I may say so, than did Jesus. Our doctrine, teaching, symbols, liturgies, say much that is important and sustaining of faith. But it is relatively rare for the church to seek to address the question of God other than from within its own world-view and language. Somehow God-talk has to make sense in the ordinary world we inhabit as well as within the room of Christian faith.

The Christian church which holds Jesus and the Christian God at its centre is diverse. It can be described denominationally in terms of Roman Catholicism, Orthodoxy, Protestantism, Pentecostalism; it contains fundamentalists who regard their own form of faith as the only form, and ecumenists who strive to gather all who can tolerate one another; doctrinally it stretches from fundamentalism through traditionalism to something like modernism. It includes those who defend the faith and those who, seeking to be true to their context, affirm black theology, the theology of liberation, feminist theology, political theology, cultural theology. It can be understood nationally or as a world faith. It is seen by those within it as an unquestioned blessing and to many outside it as truly bad news because of its repressions and domination.

So whatever I believe and have to say about Jesus and God I have always had a critical loyalty towards the church. I have felt two-footed with one foot in the church and the other firmly in the world. Although Christendom, Christianity and the Christian church are for some a dominant culture and indeed the world-view within which they want to wholly live, for me the church has only been a sub-culture. In it and through it I have been bound up in worship, fellowship, making Christians, social and political action. Within it I found my personal vocation and life's work. Because of it, being a Methodist, I have found my sense of non-conformity and dissent encouraged rather than checked. But none the less it is by no means all!

I remember years ago reading a story about a man who lived in a very attractive and beautiful place in the country. When asked to sell he said he would never sell because there he could contemplate the beauty of nature. Years later a city was built around his house until he could see nothing but cement and asphalt. But he said, 'I am not moving because I can contemplate the beauty of nature.' This, the story teller said, is what happens to the church which refuses to move and which refuses to change.

It is so long ago that I went through the doorway into the world-view which is all to do with Jesus, God and the Christian church that I can hardly imagine being anywhere else. Truly whatever my doubts, fears and criticisms I feel, mostly, at home in it. Certainly it has been for me a way to much that is important and precious. But I always remember a woman who became very much part of the life of our local church saying, 'You know, crossing the threshold into your church was one of the hardest things I ever did.'

7   Other alternatives

If I went through the doorway into the Christian faith and world-view because I was born into a Christian family then I certainly fell through some very specific doorways by being born in Britain in the twentieth century.

Some Christians, and people of other faiths, seek to live wholly within their own religious culture and world-view. Some strict Christian sects, orthodox Jews, some separatist Rastafarians, some Muslim fundamentalists all strive to live away from the world. The world and its works are basically regarded as evil, for whatever reasons, and life for the faithful is to be lived within the safety, security and purity of the ark of religious orthodoxy. Clearly this is, with varying degrees of strictness, an option.

But those of us who reject such an option have to live both within our own chosen world-view and within the overlapping world-views of society at large.

There are two reasons why I choose this second alternative. The first is that I reject the view that society and the world are evil. In other words my understanding of the world and life in terms of affirming and accepting life makes me reject the need to find an ark or separatist culture. To use traditional Christian language, if God created, redeemed and is present in the world then there is no sense in which that world can be evil in itself nor can there be any sense in which we are expected to withdraw from the world rather than engage in it.

The second is a very practical one. I cannot see how it is possible in practice to avoid being part of this secular world, with its political power and its many faiths. Even if I wanted to, its effects bite deeply into my assumptions, formation, consciousness and ways of thinking let alone into the daily externals of living and experiencing.

Strictly speaking the word secular is defined by its relation to religion and the church. That which is secular is not sacred, nor ecclesiastical, nor monastic. It is worldly and concerned with things of the world. But over the years the word secular and related words have gradually come to signify a whole world-view. It is certainly post-religious, it is also scientific and technological, it is humanistic and ethically relative. It is strongly urban, thrives on consumerism, is politically aggressive and operates on a model of constant change. In Britain it is the dominant culture and it is transmitted, I would judge, through education, the media and government, to name but three forces. Because we have a history of Christianity there is still an overlap, for example on state occasions and in relation to the monarchy, but most of the time, the underlying assumptions and direction are shaped by secularism.

There is much that is contradictory in all of this. Although religion has been pushed more into the arena of private belief vast numbers of people hold religious beliefs which in fact influence their daily lives. Although science and scientific methods are widely accepted and indeed taken for granted as the best means of explaining how the world works, scientists themselves face uncertainties and scientific understanding is so specialized that it is absorbed into public consciousness very slowly. Although the benefits of our society are clear for all who have health and money to enjoy them, the stresses and conflicts within our society are all too plain. I suspect that most of us operate with a very piecemeal and unsystematized view of what secularism is about. There will be inconsistencies. But I am saying that we live with an inadequate grasp of how this particular system works. On one level we know well enough how it works. At its best it produces marvellous inventions and technologies for 'tomorrow's world'. It finds new drugs which cure crippling diseases. It develops new high yield crops. It makes global travel ordinary. It produces nuclear energy, travels to the moon and the stars, and develops information technology of brilliant power. But at other levels I guess that most people have a fairly hazy grasp of what are the major conceptual advances which underpin and undergird this activity. Who is at home in them? Who knows their way around them? Who is teaching them and popularizing them? As I experience this world-view I find it very hard to get at those basic concepts in any ordered way. It may be that I simply do not read the right books, or watch the right TV, or read the right papers or magazines. I accept some responsibility for my own ignorance. But I think what I am pointing to is slightly different from that. It is that although the experience is thoroughgoing my ability to handle it, criticize it, be at home in it, feels somewhat limited. I wish it were otherwise.

One of the most extraordinary contradictions is that in a secular society like ours we find ourselves as the meeting place for people who belong to so many different faiths. It is not surprising that in some ways I feel more at home here because it is obviously more akin to my Christian world-view. On the other hand if it is true that in Britain people belong to a large number of different religious and ideological faiths, many of which I would regard as, to say the least, weird, then maybe the thing that is most striking is people's ability and need to find ideological faiths.

Anyhow in East London it has been possible, without claiming experience or knowledge that I do not have, to get a reasonable view of some of the world's major faiths. Just as today we can read more books, compare musical recordings, see art on many gallery walls, so here faiths meet. It is quite extraordinary to see the similarities and the differences. To see strengths and weaknesses. To see people sustained and to see corruptions within a faith-system distorting it. Let me give a few examples.

Much of my experience has been either through the personal experiences which come from living in a community which is multi-faith or through inter-faith dialogue. The first has involved us in family occasions such as weddings, turban ceremonies, festivals. The second has led us through associations of faith into visits to religious centres, talks about the faith, meeting leaders and people, sharing in meals. It has meant that we have acquired some depth of practical experience of people's faith at more than a surface or phenomenological level. Obviously this has been backed up over the years by reading. But perhaps above all it has been in moments of genuine sharing – some of which have been painful and angry – that we have begun to learn not only to see our own faith in a different way but also to begin to see the strengths of other faiths which are so strikingly different. Of course, it is impossible to separate religion from culture and so much of this dialogue has taken place against the backdrop of ethnic minority communities striving to be accepted, self-reliant and prosperous against the pressure of racism and racist violence.

For me Buddhism has made the greatest impact. Maybe because it is not one of the religions of the people of the Book and is therefore so different. It began for me in a fusty second-hand bookshop in the Lake District. Maybe it was the smell or the bargain which hooked me! Anyhow, as I have read Buddhism, and Zen Buddhism particularly, I have found a world which is fascinatingly therapeutic and challenging. It is foolish to say I have been influenced by Zen because, if I understand anything at all about it, Zen is the opposite of learning from books. But the fact is that by reading and re-reading some books over the years, and a certain amount of practice, some Zen and Buddhist ideas have come to have a direct affect on my life. I well remember some of the exhibitions I have seen on Buddhism, Japan and Tibet. So I am not so much pointing to knowledge I have acquired or can easily repeat but to some new understandings and insights which have become part of me.

But then, to give a different sort of example, people of many faiths have made a deep and lasting impact upon me. I do not just mean that I have met people who have impressed me, though that is certainly true. I mean rather that some of the people I have met have impressed me precisely because of what their faith means to them in practice. I am thinking not so much of academics I have met or even community leaders but of a few individuals and families we have got to know over the years whose lives have been shaped and formed by their faith. I also think of people I know who have been brought up within a particular faith and worldview and have rejected it because of its tradition, its rejection of the insights of the women's movement, or because of its fundamentalism. The business of living between two cultures is one that engages many young black Britons. I am often impressed by the way people strive to find and keep what is best whilst living in a modern way. Within the uncertainties and conflicts some people give a remarkable example of faithfulness and imagination.

So let me turn to my third example, political power. I choose the term because in a real sense it is what all the political systems of the world have in common. They are about the exercise of power.

In many ways I have come to an understanding and concern about politics relatively late in my life. I was, I regret to say, quite apolitical for much of my life. I have come to it because our life in East London over the last decade or so and our experience of the inner-city have forced it upon me.

As in speaking of secularism, I would say that I have only a very piecemeal understanding of the world of politics and economics.

Nonetheless I am compelled to take it very seriously indeed. On a world scale we see issues such as massive poverty, hunger and the threat of extending wars. At home we live with a society which has, I believe, indisputably become more divided and where a modified class system and social stratification still rule supreme. This is not the place to rehearse all the statistics and reports but they show that a growing number and proportion of citizens do not have, by any normal standards, a reasonable quality of life, let alone share in what for some is a quickly growing prosperity. The contrast between the poor in Britain and the world of consumer capitalism which can be seen on any TV adverts or in any newly-built shopping precinct or hypermarket is alarming. It is difficult to find adequate words to express what is happening, but for some people there is personal alienation, there is economic exploitation which results in the weakest and the most needy being pushed to the wall, there is the use of political power and political systems which leads to domination rather than to freedom for all.

Of course, power politics contain opposing elements. I believe there is something fundamentally unfair and unjust in the capitalist system. It is based on greed, competitiveness, and the abuse of the majority by the minority who find themselves with power, wealth and privilege. My knowledge of socialism, let alone Marxism, is patchy and inadequate, but there are certain aspects of them which seem to me to make sense of what is happening in our world. Compared with my motivation and commitment to Jesus this is a small influence on my life. But I know that in the terms that I do understand, justice, peace, love, freedom, collectiveness, there are aspects of political power which I will oppose. There is an unfairness which is wrong. There is an injustice which steals the world's wealth and resources for the few. And whether it be the few countries, or a few transnational corporations, a few families or a few individuals, such misuse of power has to be challenged.

These are all examples of what I am calling alternative world-views. All of us live within them to a greater or lesser extent. If we are committed to one particular world-view then alternative world-views are either to be avoided or handled with care.

8 Money and work

We seem to be developing more and more into a society in which money, and all the more sophisticated forms of money, dominate. Clearly there is something obvious in the argument that wealth has to be created for a society to have sufficient to meet all its needs. But often no one really questions who in fact (as individuals, groups or countries) pays the price and to what extent it all happens at other people's expense or the expense of the earth's limited resources. Also money seems to be becoming more and more dominating in the sense that profit and the ability to pay have become the only criteria. This has become not simply a matter of how our economic affairs are organized but of the way we are shaping society. This focus on money and profit shapes the values with which people relate to each other, because if all that matters is profit and securing money and wealth then the values of competitiveness, strength, ruthlessness, acquisitiveness, and the sheer use of power become alone important.

Almost everything in our society needs money. The only people who are likely to disagree are those who have so much money that they have forgotten or never known what it is like not to be able to do things without money. For some people it means going hungry, being cold in winters, only buying second-hand clothes and constantly being dependant upon a small weekly income from the state. For others it means being denied those modern basics and consumer goods which everyone with money takes for granted. For some it means never having a holiday. For some, of course, in developing countries, it means a life which is almost entirely on the fringe of the world of money. There is no doubt that money is the key which increases the number of options that are open to people. I know from my own first hand experience, when we had not enough money to pay fuel bills or when we feared the slightest repair bill to our car, how the lack of money worries and depresses. It is not a large step to begin to realize what it must be like for those who are constantly on low pay or on no pay at all. Indeed, through our church community work over the years I have been able to see a little of people in very serious straits. I have seen in people I know quite well and care about how the lack of money debilitates, de-skills, confuses. I have seen how easily it leads to illness and breakdown.

It is quite interesting going into a bank. The bank presents itself as modern, efficient, high-tech. You queue, stand at a counter with all the security precautions in evidence, you are aware that part of the teller's job is to make sure you are not, in some way, cheating. You know, especially when you do not have much money, that the politeness and service lasts so long as your computer statement is in credit. The whole transaction, in fact, rests on the assumption that you have money. This is obvious. But I make the point because this service facility which we take for granted is either denied to those with little money or it becomes, I am sure, a place of stress and confusion.

Sometimes when I go into central London, perhaps to an art gallery, I find myself walking through some of the wealthier shopping arcades or streets. The sheer range of goods available is astonishing even by the reasonable standards I am used to. The prices are excessive and beyond what I could imagine paying for shoes, a shirt, for some luxury item or a present. The gap between such shops, even allowing for the tourist market, and the world of the inner city is almost too great to comprehend. What it must be like compared with the poverty of the developing third world I cannot really imagine. So part of the reality that money represents is the disparity between sections of our society. Some people argue that this is how it has always been, and that in any case the needs of the poor can only ever be met through the creation of wealth. Others wonder how such extremes can be contained within one social fabric without it tearing apart.

Yet I know that there are individuals and organizations whose wealth and power far exceeds what I see at street level. Occasionally the wealth and power of the very rich and the transnational companies is evident for all to see. What I think is hard to handle, in so far as it actually affects my life, is that this reality in fact has a direct effect on us and our lives and yet we are almost totally powerless. It is interesting within normal political argument, let alone at election time, how little mention is ever made as to who benefits from the profits made in the money markets of the world. Nor is it often explained who is exploited, who pays the price, or who suffers.

If money is the means to get options and increase the range of choices, then for most of us having a job is the means to get money. The rise in unemployment during these last years has therefore been a serious and continuing tragedy. I will not rehearse the statistics which show how those who are unemployed are much more likely to be physically ill, or in psychiatric hospitals, or to die at an early age. This is no surprise to anyone who understands how poverty and lack of work diminish and destroy people.

But my own life has not been like this. I have worked since I was twenty-three years old as a Methodist minister and this has carried with it, for good and ill, the provision of a tied house. I wonder sometimes what it would be like to do an ordinary job. I remember what it felt like when for short periods I worked as a postman, in a textile clothlooking department, as a labourer on a factory roof, and as a nurse in the sick ward of a psychiatric hospital.

Over the years I have tried to structure the work which is such an important part of my life and which has the tendency to take over the whole of my waking hours. So in order to contain it to reasonable hours I have tried to adapt some of the skills used in other jobs so as to analyse, assess and evaluate my work. Part of this, of course, has required consultation with other colleagues. Anyhow this method of job analysis has helped me make a distinction between the demands of my vocation and the requirements of a job of work.

But the greatest pressure on my work has been that the role of being a minister, cleric, priest has been under such threat over the years. This has come partly through belonging to a declining institution. It has also come about as new disciplines and jobs have cut into the traditional roles of the clergy. This has meant some have felt that they have been left either with the residue of a job or an impossible job. For some this has become an impossible stress leading to breakdown in health, marriage or moral conduct. Because I have been able to sort out my own strengths and weaknesses, because I have been able to find ways of monitoring my work, and above all because of lively and committed colleagueship, it is many years since I wanted to resign! It is worth saying that I frequently did want to resign for the first thirteen years! So from within my odd job I have this limited understanding of pressure and stress. I know through many people I meet something of the pressures of work which lead to redundancy, illness, and breakdown as well as to that heaven on earth which comprises a large house in a commuter village, a superlative car and at least two holidays abroad a year. When thinking of unemployment and changes in industry it is important not to forget just how many people have had their lives changed by work. People who worked in coal mines, like my wife's father, often coughed their lungs out or died young. People who worked in the textile industry, which our family knew, found themselves with damaged hands and arthritis caused by the artificially created atmosphere. It is not right to be nostalgic about these old days when working conditions were often so bad and so unhealthy. Today it is worth watching out for the extent to which those in low pay jobs pay a high price for their wages in damage to health.

One image stays with me. It illustrates both industrial changes and changes in the underlying political decisions. The textile industry was told that if the old Lancashire looms were broken up and new automatic looms bought then some compensation would be given. I can see it now. A weaving shed that was normally racing with noise and energy, big as several football pitches, was covered with heaps of broken weaving frames.

So money and work are indeed of the raw materials of my life. In more recent years government, commercialism, society have begun to develop options for leisure. For most people with money, increased leisure and new opportunities for leisure must surely be good news. People spend time in do-it-yourself house repairs, gardening or fishing. They join clubs and associations, of which there are an endless variety. And our society strives to discover what it means for people who will spend a major part of their lives not working. It wrestles with the whole idea of work, leisure, retirement. It struggles with the very different interests of individuals and communities and the needs of consumer capitalism.

If money and work have to be understood both personally and politically it has become increasingly clear that sex and sexuality also have personal and political dimensions.

9 Sex and sexuality

I sometimes think that the single most important thing that happens to us is whether we are born male or female. In some societies female children are still killed because they are unwanted. In most societies women are discriminated against and have far less power than men. It is a striking fact of our society that changes towards equality for women in voting, employment, legal status and rights have all needed to be hard fought. The slightest glance at what is happening in society shows how far there is to go yet.

My understanding of this perception has come about mainly because my wife and partner is a feminist. It has meant for us a continuous assessment and even negotiation of how our marriage works. It has meant that I have learnt not only to see the point of using inclusive language, of learning to exchange roles in child-rearing, but that I have discovered a more flexible understanding of masculinity and femininity than the one I grew up with. The recognition that so many of my assumptions are in fact prejudices and unnecessarily restricting has gradually become real for me. This of course influences how I see other people and not least how I see and relate to women. But the major change is in how I see myself.

When I was a teenager I was reasonably good at sport and played a lot of football, cricket, table tennis, and went cross-country running. It was much later that I realized I was a nine-stone weakling who wore glasses and preferred reading books to almost anything else! Maybe I never felt threatened by a macho-image, as we now call it, because I did not know of it. What I somehow did not uncover, not even with the help of the largish teenage group I belonged to, was any conscious or articulated understanding of how maleness and femaleness contribute to the make-up of each person.

I think I have also learnt that there is an important, though over-lapping, distinction to be made between gender and sexuality. Given that we are male or female and that we acknowledge our masculinity and femininity, each of us has to own and accept our own sexuality. By this I mean that sexual feelings, desires, emotions, thoughts, dreams, actions are all part of what each one of us is as a separate person. In this important sense sexuality is not only to do with relationships with other people. It is also very much to do with what we are as whole people.

Let me try to explain with two examples.

It is surprising within most art galleries and art exhibitions how little is to do with sex and sexuality. But occasionally in an exhibition a picture or a sculpture has something in it which is erotic for the viewer. Now I do not suppose for a moment that most of us viewing such a painting or sculpture would consciously make any distinction between its aesthetic, artistic or sexual appeal. Its beauty, sensuality, physicalness, eroticism all merge. I use the example because I think this is close to how we are as people. This is what it is like to describe our own sexuality. Though it is in a real sense a separate part of us it is one element within our personality and one factor in our response to the world around us.

Sometimes we meet another person and find ourselves disproportionately attracted to them. If we think about it we can no doubt find reasons why we like them but in truth the attraction goes beyond any rationalization. Sometimes when this happens the two people sooner or later become partners. Sometimes they have a friendship within which overt sexuality may or may not be excluded. I use this example because I know that single people, gay and homosexual friends, married people, all attest this experience. There is a lovely incident in a novel where a man is attracted by a woman's looks and follows her without ever seeing her properly. He watches her buy flowers, he notices her clothes, her poise. And, as she turns, he realizes it is his own wife and that he has seen her, as it were, for the first time.

So these raw materials of gender and sexuality are important. Without some positive understanding of them it is likely that our sexual lives will be less fulfilling than they could be.

In our society and within much of the church there are so many negatives to do with sex. The church in this century has found it difficult to sort out its moral teaching. A great deal of the whole church's teaching is still based on the idea that sex is bad and wrong unless it is for producing children. This is a crude way for me to state such a complicated subject but I think at the last analysis this is what is actually going on. In fairness to the church, society still retains some very negative attitudes and teaching about sex. But the church, on the whole, has found it difficult to separate out its understanding of the value of sex in itself, the responsibility of people to each other, the opportunity to control family size through contraception, the changing patterns of family life and child rearing, and its criticism of relationships, of all kinds, which are exploitative or even violent.

There are some real negatives to be taken into account. The arguments rage of course as to how these are defined and controlled. Society gives fairly complicated messages to young people on many things. I would think the messages regarding sex are even more complicated than most. In families, schools, church or mosque, on TV conflicting and contradictory ideas and pictures to do with sex are given. In one sense sex is normal and natural. In another it is hidden. In one sense sex is within a loving and caring relationship, in another it always seems best with someone else. Sex is normal but competitive. It is intended to be pleasurable but it is sometimes to do with violence. All these and more crossed messages exist. At an extreme, though where that extreme is set is again part of the argument, society says that some sexual behaviour should not be seen in public or on TV, it even says that some is illegal, pornographic, or has, to use the old phrase, a 'tendency to deprave or corrupt'. There is a whole mesh of negatives in society which exist quite separately from a couple's own experiences and satisfaction from sex.

It is very strange that in spite of all the openness about sex we have not begun to find a way through to a much more positive understanding of sex. The AIDS disease has of course only swung us back towards a view of sex as being to do with negatives and problems. But I think underneath this lies the deeper question of why it is that as humans we are not more able to discover satisfaction and fulfilment with less hurt, disruption, breakdown. What is going on in a society when sex becomes so much to do with fragmented relationships, ill health and even with sexual violence?

I recall the article which firmly committed me to the distinction between talking about sex and talking about sexual violence. So much that is to do with crime, in the rape and murder of women, so much that is to do with serious sexual deviation, pathology and extreme pornography is in fact to do with sexual violence.

And yet sex is much more to do with positive pleasure and a

loving relationship. There is a proper sense of privacy and intimacy about it. It is precisely because such experiences are of such worth and of such openness that we speak of them carefully in a whisper rather than shout about them in a competitive way. I would say that there is not enough sensuality or eroticism in our society. Certainly if there were more open, positive sensuality and eroticism shown within loving relationships then, I believe, there would be less shame, guilt, embarrassment, and less sexual violence. Somehow we have to find the way to communicate all this more clearly.

So with such an understanding of gender, sexuality and sex, I have to face the real world our children inhabit. If there is one point at which the generation gap becomes a chasm it is in relation to sex. For some people sex, before the advent of AIDS, had become as ordinary and matter of fact as conversation, and the charge of promiscuity seemed quite inappropriate. No one would accuse someone of being promiscuous or mistaken in having many friends! The question is whether or not sex in itself needs when practised between people rather than singly to be relational. If it does then the decision to be promiscuous or even to have a succession of partners is not primarily to do with sex but, at a more fundamental level, to do with our perception of relationships. In the same way the question of what happens to us as people when we have unloving, or uncaring, or even violent sex is as much if not more to do with us as people as it is about our sexual frustration or satisfaction.

Underneath the question of the quality of our relationships, is the question of how we understand and value faithfulness and loyalty to other people. I say this, with the clear recognition that for many people, and for all of us potentially, relationships can and do go wrong and have to end. But the search for faithfulness and loyalty, which is not only to do with duration of time, is crucial in our understanding of gender, sexuality and sex itself.

10 Being creative

There are very many ways of being creative. There is something vitally attractive in trying to be original, inventive, imaginative. Whatever form it takes it has about it real energy. The act of truly creating something, whatever its value to other people, is exciting and stimulating. Somehow the process enhances the person doing the creating. Somehow it intensifies that person's identity and at best enhances their sense of self-affirmation and self-determination. Some believe it is to do with properly using both the left and right sides of the brain.

Books, films and TV, art and drawing, music, writing are things which are important to me and which I could spend my life on. Quite happily I could settle down with them and find satisfaction and refreshment. The whole range of people's creativity is so vast that I doubt anyone could find their way round all of it. The challenge to be creative yourself is likewise endless. However inadequately you work, whether or not your work is seen let alone valued by others, once you start to write, or write poetry, or draw, or make music, or whatever it is, you find yourself pulled into these new and satisfying worlds. If it only depended on fame or success then most of us would stop tomorrow.

When I write, like this, or write poems, draw, or paint I find myself having to go through several barriers. As always there are questions about whether I can in fact do what I want to do. There are questions as to whether I am doing it for myself or to be seen by others. But these are passing problems. Once I get down to writing or drawing, let us say, I find a tremendous sense of release. If I am in the mood, if I can write or draw directly then I find it immensely satisfying. It is as though the poem I write or the lines I draw come directly from me. There is no gap between the experiences or object and myself. There is no gap between what I want to say or draw and how I do it. I have always written and done poems over the years but when I started drawing again, at my fortieth birthday, I felt as though I had found an important part of myself that I had switched off. Sometimes I copy, sometimes I draw from life, sometimes I do my own imaginatives which at their best come with this immediacy and directness.

But writing and drawing are not the only part of this raw material of being creative because I am able to see and learn from other people's creativity. Some people find this through music, opera, ballet, the theatre, painting and sculpture, films and TV, books and literature, gardening, cooking, crafts: the list is a very long one.

Two main ones get under my skin. Even though I read quite a

lot and would count reading as one of my main pleasures I find watching TV, and in particular films, quite consuming. I secondly find art through painting and sculpture endlessly interesting and stimulating. These ways into reality are so available. They invite me to join in their creativity and they provide opportunities for me to respond creatively to them.

I think that of all of them films and TV have had the most direct effect on my life. I will not recount the stories of the last fifty that have impressed me! When I was young and people went to the cinema I used to walk to our church on a Sunday morning with a cousin. I always used to tell her, so she says, the story of the film I had seen at the cinema the night before. I did this in great and preferably gory detail. As so many others have said there is a particular sense of expectancy as the lights go down and the so real unreality begins. I know that watching films and TV can actually engage my concentration and commitment to a very high degree. Of course I know the difference between material that is solely for modest entertainment and that which I would regard as of real worth. I can be critical, analytical, selective. I can even, if threatened, switch a film off! Out of this constant flow of images, stories, characters, experiences, emotion I have taken many things: information, pleasure, the opportunity to escape and to try out in safety what I could not possible do in reality, and, most seriously, an opportunity to see the development of a wholly new art form which has only existed within the years of this century.

Painting and sculpture involve us, in some ways, in a more public creativity because in addition to seeing them in books, or cuttings and reproductions, we can go to galleries and share in a public event. The galleries are themselves part of the creativity on offer. There are very modern ones, commercial galleries, the great national collections, smaller galleries for a town or around a particular artist, there are museums, there are even buildings which are themselves exhibits of the work of their architects. Each has its own feel, expectation, involvement with the commercial side of art. I know as I go into them that there is much between me and the artist but I go and look and find myself bored, shocked, excited, stimulated. So I return from such visits wanting to learn about the artist. I look up references in books or my scrap book collection. I find myself even writing about them, arguing about them with people I have shared the experience with, looking out for programmes about the artist on TV.

Let me try to illustrate what creativity means to me from this art perspective.

I remember when our children were quite small going to an exhibition of very modern sculpture which comprised flat tiles, arrangements of bricks, arrangements of wood. Whilst we were looking round the artist came up to us and asked us if we liked his work. There was the contrast between this man's gentleness towards our two small children and the way the newspapers ridiculed his work and the galleries which paid money for it. There was also the sheer fact of meeting a famous artist. At this quite naive level we were somehow involved in the process.

I think of exhibitions I was taken to by other people when I did not expect to find anything I valued. I recall for example an amazing one by three modern architects, another of art nouveau jewellery, some photographic ones. There is really something astonishingly good to be surprised by pleasure. Not only does it do something for the relationship with the person who took you but it also releases in you ideas, feelings, preferences and prejudices which you did not know about.

Sometimes an exhibition can be exciting in a very positive way. We were confronted by a very large number of paintings and their impact was far greater than we expected. Not only were we seeing originals with all their colour, intensity and plasticity but we were seeing so many of them that the sheer energy, vitality, vigour, output of the painter became in itself a contribution to the experience.

Again there are times when a painter's vision of the world is so bleak and so grim that you find yourself having to leave. It is quite extraordinary to feel, yes these paintings are brilliant, yes I really like them and admire what he is attempting to do, but I cannot remain with them any longer or I shall be overcome by their vision of humanity, by their pain, distortion, isolation, cagedness. I remember after such an exhibition a friend and I sat drinking coffee, silent for the best part of half an hour, before we could find the words to begin to explore what we had felt.

So this is a little of the excitment and energy I find in other people's art and in other people's films. I work at the same task of being creative through my own writing and drawing. You have to make your own witness and your own statement about what the world is like to you. We have to use our experiences and those we share and those which overlap with other people. We have to shape them and form them by ourselves and from within ourselves. Sometimes we do this for ourselves and sometimes we do it for people we love. Somehow we have to find the balance and poise to be creative. So we go to an art gallery, or we listen to music, or we watch a film or TV, we read the literature, join the dance, see the carnival, pick the flowers, share our love. We can be caught up in poems and words, in pictures, in photographs. In a very deep way our attempts to be creative now in an intense present are both a contract with our past and a promise to the future and our children. We hope that our creativity will be a transcending experience for others as well as for ourselves. In such creativity we find not only the raw material of our art form but also part of the substance and depth of our lives.

11 Inner space

All the time, wherever we are and whatever we do, we bang up against everything that is on the outside of our skin! The sheer noise that comes from all the external demands is quite deafening. Most of the time we do not listen. Information pours in. People constantly make demands upon us, a flow of people streaming from an underground station at rush hour or down a street in India, or one person in eye to eye contact. Always we have to find satisfactory ways of relating to what is around us. We have at least to be able to survive if not to be fulfilled within it. Sometimes we choose to live or have to live where the level of stress and conflict is very high. But all of us have to make some sort of trade off or contract between ourselves and the world outside.

I do not know whether or not it is sensible to live in an earthquake zone or on the fertile slopes of an active volcano, but people do. People also live in the inner city as we do, and find there that it is a place of almost unlimited frontiers. And where frontiers meet it is difficult to keep yourself safely. At frontiers you need passports and guile. You need many languages and the capacity to be chameleons and change quickly. You need to have a firm hold on

yourself and all your precious baggage. You need a sure eye for the
authorities which police such places and make them safe by putting up barbed wire and planting minefields. Frontier people have
to accept the reality of uncertainty. They know something of the
worlds that are changing around them. We all have to find some
inner space. There are different ways to talk about this and they
can be reached, for example, through religion, humanistic psychology, literature, Zen, existentialism, lateral thinking, to name but a
few.

But whatever I have learned and go on learning from such I
have a sense of my own inner space which is very much one of the
raw materials of my life. It is part of me as a person and it is the
very opposite end to the experience of being crowded by all that is
around me. The idea and image is a very powerful one because it
suggests that as a person I am a complex entity within which are
vast unknowns. I find this attractive rather than frightening. It
makes me feel that there are places to be explored. It makes me
remember occasions when I have gone into my inner space, when
I have felt at home in myself, when I have been focussed, rooted
and fulfilled. It also makes me recall times when I have been off
balance and when I have experienced the threat of breaking down
because I have felt diseased, timid, depressed, overwhelmed or
overstretched. So within my skin there is, to use a different image,
an ecological system which I understand inadequately and yet
from which I expect a great deal. Within it, as a focus, is 'me'. If
I am in pain it is difficult to separate me from whatever and
wherever that pain is centred. If I am happy and active then I am
in the words which flow within my head, in the centre of stillness
between my eyes, in the deep space of silence within myself, and
in the actions of my life.

There is a whole bagfull of words that I have picked up, mostly
I think from humanistic psychology, and they mean a lot to me.
They are shorthand ways of describing what it means to live as a
human being in a way that is positive, in a way that has freed itself
from pathology, artificiality, defensiveness, anxiety. They are
about ways of living and acting which flow from us when we are
truly at home within ourselves and within our inner space. They
are the opposite of all those existentialist anxieties which once pur-
sued me through adolescence, novels and films. They are the

opposite of madness. The list includes words like autonomy, aware-ness, spontaneity, intimacy, authenticity, self-transcendence and self-realization.

Let me give an ordinary and external example which I have experienced many times. It applies I know to many sports and activities but I will use the example of playing table tennis. The point I want to focus on is the common fact that sometimes within a game, and against the same player, you can move from playing badly to playing well. At one point all is effort, miss hits, near misses, the usual bad shots. At another, suddenly, effortlessly, shots go in, reflexes and intuition take over, well practised strokes come off. At best you cease to think or feel and you, the bat, the ball and the table tennis table become one movement and one action.

So it is and so it can be with our whole lives. I know people who play like this and are like this, if not all the time, at least for much of the time. Such a way of living and being I find impossible to attain. Or more properly, I know I need to strive effortlessly if I am ever to find how to be like this. I know that in order to have any hope of being like this, out there (at the frontiers, with the noise, with all the demands, with all the stress, pressures and con-flicts), I have to find ways of being like this, within myself.

There are a number of overlapping ways through which this has made some sense to me. At varying levels what I am talking about is present in much of what I have already described as the raw materials of my life. As you might expect these overlap untidily. So to speak of my ordinary life, the people in it, to speak of my work, of sexuality and sex, of being creative is already to point to some of those things which nurture me within my inner space. But there are some more specific actions.

There are very many different methods and disciplines which are intended to help people go into themselves. There are many ways of travelling into your own inner space. I must say I have a bad habit of reading how such methods work rather than practis-ing making them work. But I know people, for example, who find relaxation, yoga, meditation, physical disciplines enormously liberat-ing. Other people listen to music. Others grow plants. Others say their prayers and use religious objects and words to develop their devotion and self-awareness. It is quite clear that people use very different methods and even techniques to get to the same place: within themselves.

For myself, when I am not exercising to prevent my back or shoulders seizing up, I engage in a very simple form of meditation and relaxation. I do not know what happens to other people but for me this simple method of lying on the ground, concentrating on my breathing, trying gently to see and feel and sense what is within me, is a very good experience. So good that I must be an idiot not to do it more often! Always it makes me feel better. Sometimes I see the most wonderful colours. Sometimes I believe I find a stillness which is wholly right.

Once all of this happened to me quite unexpectedly and in a way that was wholly out of proportion. Shortly after the children were born and, no doubt suffering from sleep-interrupted nights, I went on a training course to do with my job. It was at Ambleside in the Lake District and, though February, it was a time of bright sunshine. Part of the course used simple encounter group experiences. It was within that unlikely situation that I took what, up to now, has been my furthest or most intense journey into inner space. I remember I was looking at a beautiful heraldic window with broken panes. I felt a beam of light and quietness which felt to be quite other than from the sunshine. I felt my blood through my finger tips like waves beating, I heard a waterfall in the distance and as I continued to share in the 'group life' I felt this immense quietness. I could not explain it. It felt physical. It continued after the group session had finished through the afternoon and into the next session. It was as though the quietness within me were as physical and complete as any solid thing could be. Afterwards it made me strive and dig within myself to find adequate words to share what had happened to me. But the quietness I had experienced – and this is a dozen years ago – opened up for me and in me the awareness that there are depths within me, and journeys within me and places within me, that I have not yet begun to understand or explore. It was wholly the opposite to what people describe as out of body experiences.

So when I speak of inner space as a raw material I have both some ordinary and one extraordinary experience to go on. But though it is important to see this journey within ourselves as something in itself I know that for most of the time there is a fierce and energetic interchange between my life and actions and my inner self. In addition to the raw materials I have already mentioned I find that anything which increases my intensity of awareness, anything which enhances my capacity to see and feel and know, is part of this process. It is present in creativity, in insight, in humour, in lateral thinking, in self-transcendence. It is even present when, in engaging in social and political action, we so overreach ourselves in struggling for justice and right that we realize the sheer nowness of our own human existence.

12 Inner city

If I have learnt that inner space matters to me it is certainly true that in the decade or so that we have lived in East London I have learned just how much a place, situation and context matter. We moved to East London because of our work and because we wanted the opportunity to live in a multi-racial, multi-cultural and multi-faith neighbourhood. We have through our work got into the wider reality which is described as the inner city. The inner city is not only a geographical or sociological location, it has also become a political reality.

Without claiming too much for our own experience I know the extent to which this place has impressed us. It is difficult to overstate its effect on me or to overvalue how it has changed and modified my perception both of myself and the world. It is important to see and understand why and in what ways the place we are in shapes us. I have seen what it has done to me. I have seen, when in our work we have tried to share the problems of the inner city with people in suburbia, the staggering gap which exists. The 1987 election only underlined this experience of division. In a sense this gap is a witness to the truth that where you are shapes and directs what you are.

Here is how I described Stratford when I first knew it in 1976. I am going to use this old description, rather than compile a new one, because I still remember, and sometimes recapture, the sheer excitement of those first months. If you go out of our small church in Stratford you can see a hospital, a school, a police station, some houses. By walking about two hundred yards you cross a major six-lane road which goes into the city and you find yourself in a shopping precinct, which leads to a market, to bus, underground and rail stations. If you climb the stairs or go in the lift to the top of the multi-storey car park you can see a vast industrial area with an international freight terminal for container traffic, you can see the housing estates which include so many high rise flats, you can see London with its seven million people stretching into the distance. If you look at our bit of it, say 40,000 people, you can see many good things and many bad things. People come here and talk about problems. Certainly people in high rise flats have problems of poor community facilities, people being shut off, rubbish not being collected, vandalism and violence, lifts going out of order. Certainly inner city areas as a whole have problems of comparatively poor housing, education, employment opportunities and so on. All this is true, and I am sure that people who are less privileged than I am, that is those who do not have a nice home in which to shelter, a car in which to move around, a phone with which to contact people, some money to spare, find the difficulties to be overwhelming. But it is not fanciful to say that there is also a great life and liveliness in the inner city. To walk through the market, if you can cope with watching the live eels being cut up, is, as in any market, to share in a world of vigour and energy. To go to the local theatre to a pantomime is to see theatre given a local touch. To support West Ham at football . . . is not always easy! To go into Asian or Caribbean shops or homes, to meet African students or Malaysian Chinese nurses is to travel the world. People live in the inner city for many reasons, and when you see all the groups, leisure activities, community organizations, you get a glimpse both of the fragmented nature of the city and its potency. 'All human life is there' and at times it feels it.

Let me illustrate this even more personally. For some eleven years I had to drive from Newham down to our office at the Bow Mission. This takes you over the Bow flyover. There have been days when, even as I have been stuck on the flyover in congested traffic, I have felt elated by the city. All around there are houses, buildings and flats, to the south the motorway goes towards the new Docklands, with all its mixed benefits for local people, to the north the motorway goes towards canals and railways. Overhead there is a plane or a helicopter.

We had a mural of the city painted on the wall of one of our church buildings. The artist started work and on the first day someone stole the scaffolding, so we had some sharp conversations about who ought to have insured it! It is about as large as the side of a house. You can see it, in its retouched colours, from the nearby high rise flats. There is a door through it into the doctor's surgery and the people going in see it. The background is of geometric shapes. The colours, even now they have been repainted, are gentle, striking but not gaudy. The mural is all about people. There are people in cars and mending them, children playing, workers working, sick people waiting, a clown clowning, a mother feeding a baby, youngsters dancing, old people standing talking. I have so often gone round the corner from my office to stand and to look at it. It gives me that same elation that I sensed on the flyover.

I remember one day, when our children were small enough to need carrying, I lifted them up to a window for their first look at live eels. The man suddenly, and quite unexpectedly, chopped them, live and bleeding, into pieces. At another market, years later, we watched an eel poke its head, like a snake, over the edge of its tray. Suddenly, it reared up, like a grass snake at my fear of touching, and dropped into the gutter under the stall where in a trickle of water it moved towards a grate. A small boy with a gun was watching and said to the stall holder, 'Hey mister your eel's escaped'. 'Better shoot it then' said the man, as he picked it up and put it back into the tray.

The inner city is a place of great problems, many of which are not of its making. It is a place in which I have found that unless you have some working understanding of power and politics you have little with which to judge what is happening around you. In the inner city such political sense becomes as natural as breathing. Even within a relatively conservative institution like the church the sheer hurt, waste and pain caused by Thatcherism is acknowledged and criticized. I suspect that for most of us living in the inner city the issues, for much of the time, are too big and too remote and often too debilitating for us to respond adequately. People under extreme stress make misjudgments, behave violently, have even a tendency to do things against their own long term self-interests. One writer calls it a fear of freedom, and it is a terrible thing. As I write I am listening to some exquisite music and the contrast, the frustration, the anger I feel at the waste of people trickles in tears down my cheeks. To fear freedom, to fail to kick open the door when you can, to lose the opportunity to get, even in small measure, out of the chains and restriction is very hard to bear. And yet we see this, in people, all the time.

The problems, especially of poverty, have been extraordinarily well documented. The reasons for the poverty, whether on the relative scale of East London or the absolute scale of those countries where people starve to death, is quite clear. It is because those of us who are comfortably off are not willing to change either our personal or institutional conduct so as to help. There are more complex arguments. We argue according to our political and economic theories. But the raw material of my life now contains the belief, however explained, that the comfortable, the rich, the wealthy, steal (such a crude word for such sophisticated dealings) the world's resources and use them for their own ends. In doing so they steal from others, who because of this remain poor. I know the analysis terrifies me. But it is the only one that fits the reality and I would rather be terrified than deny the truth of what I see. It is there in individuals whom we strive to help, it is there in disadvantaged systems and institutions, it is there in international affairs. And before it, and it is something you really learn to understand in the inner city, you feel powerless and helpless. But you still try to do something to change it.

So living here has irreversibly changed my view of the world. Because of the people with whom I live and work I see myself differently. It is not simply a question of who shares in prosperity and who does not. It is not that if we only all had enough money then we would all vote Conservative. It is more a question of what sort of humans and what sort of society we are seeking to build. One world development writer has defined power as the power of A to do to B what B cannot do to A. That is spot on. I have learnt in the inner city to strive to change this imbalance of power and to question any power which is weighted. We have to ask whether we are working for a society which is based on and encourages ruthlessness, acquisitiveness and power or one that is caring, compassionate, inventive, imaginative and where people can be responsibly independent.

Certainly in the inner city I find myself straining after a freedom which is beyond me. It is beyond me in the sense that I cannot hope to attain it. It is also beyond me because I am part of it only by virtue of having taken sides with those who are suffering. They have been described world wide as the oppressed, they are denied their own true humanity, they are exploited, they are what one writer has called the wretched of the earth. By making space for people, by taking sides, by standing in other people's shoes, by practising disinterested compassion, we find ourselves stretched to the limits. Those limits lie close to the surface in our British inner cities.

13   Moral values

In using the word, image, symbol of raw materials I said at the outset that raw materials can be mixed together in different ways. So when I come now to consider moral values I am in no way suggesting that I have not been concerned with moral values so far, because I have.

Underlying so much of what I am trying to share is a vision and a passion for justice, peace and love. If we value people, if we see our common humanity, then nothing less than peace through justice makes any kind of lasting sense. To say this, in our world, means that unless we are strong and careful we are likely to be overwhelmed by failure, if not our own failure then that of the world. But if we can control our hope, if we can formulate our visions in words and actions which really do aim for the end we seek, then we can be part of the process of change. So both in my personal quest and in my engagement with issues of humanity and society I care about all that creates, builds up and grows and I am opposed to all that breaks down, destroys and diminishes. I am against everything that oppresses, belittles, ensnares, chains, makes impotent. I want freedom from all dominations because I see them as blocks to us being the people and societies we can be, are meant to be, and are most fulfilled in being.

Such a single-minded understanding of moral values does not, of course, mean that there are not hard decisions when seeking to apply these values to real situations. Of course not. But it does mean that I have a rule of thumb, guidelines, game-rules which are portable. To seek to be creating, life affirming and life building, in terms of justice, peace and love, can be spelt out in real situations. For example, we are to take a preferential option for the poor for how else can their pain and suffering be relieved? We are to work for real equality of opportunity for people in education, for how else will all be valued? We are to feed the world, for if we do not our own humanity is at risk; we are to practice love, a love for people that can be described as disinterested because its focus is the need of others, compassionate because it touches and changes the one who seeks to express it, tough because it is not unblinkered to the responsibility of anyone.

Let me give three more lengthy examples.

Over these last twenty years I have been involved with the struggle for racial justice in Britain. We have come to use the word racism to point to all the complex ways that the white system and white people collude in and practice this discrimination, disadvantaging and violence against the ethnic minority communities in Britain. In other countries different situations are found. Other words are needed to describe how power is used and how communities conflict. But I do not believe that pointing to the terrible conflict between other groups (be they Sinhalese and Tamil, Hindu and Muslim, Protestant and Catholic, Iraqi and Iranian) lessens the grim story of white racism which has spread across the world because of Europe's imperial history. Nor for that matter is their violence any more human simply because it is not described as racism.

We humans have a very long history of hating and killing. We also have a long history of dominating other peoples, treating them unfairly and doing violence to them. It is impossible to speak of justice, peace and love without acknowledging these realities. The problems constantly hit you in the face. There is the sheer, persistent and perverse insensitivity between individuals. There is the constant failure to do anything to redress unequal opportunities and to abolish privilege in so many institutions and systems. And, not least, there is the horrific catalogue of violence from our wars.

I have found over the years that the search for racial justice leads to a search for all human rights and for thorough-going political rights. The search for racial justice concerns the whole society because it is a mirror and test to the quality and health of the whole society. If this is detailed in terms of any minority group and their rights I would say that minorities should have the same human and legal rights as everyone else; that they should have the right to fulfil their own particular needs; that they should have the right to be different; but, speaking from within the United Nations Declaration on Human Rights in 1948, they do not have the right to oppress other people. So I have found that the search for racial justice has led me to a concern for all minority rights and indeed for all human rights. The search for racial justice leads us through a commitment to social action to a commitment to political justice. You begin with being concerned about justice for ethnic minorities and you end caring about justice for all people. You start, as I found so long ago, with race and end with politics.

I was one of the people who believed we were not only mistaken but morally wrong to go to war over the Falklands. As the events of 1982 unfolded I found myself entirely caught out. Never before in my adult lifetime had we been at war. Never before had I realized how quickly people could decide that causing other people to die was acceptable. I am not going to rehearse the complex arguments about the reasons for the war, though I did at the time take it all very seriously. The point of using this as an example is that I find our capacity for violence, without ever working through all the preliminary options, breathtaking. I am not for a moment saying Argentina was in the right, nor am I commenting on the complex historical background which was the basis for the conflict. What I am saying is that in that situation a person who believes in being life-affirming, creating, life-building had to speak out against such destruction and killing. And yet of course, as a citizen, I was part of it.

My third example is to do with Jesus of the Gospels. It is here also that Jesus becomes part of the raw material of my life. By this I mean that studying, reading, teaching, discussing the Jesus of the Gospels has become for me as much a part of my moral values as any other direct experience. Some years ago I edited a Christian magazine which had a special combined issue on spirituality and politics. Here is how I described the Jesus of the Gospels whom I saw then and see now as informing so much of the moral values I accept. Here, I said, you will see Jesus. He is in our experiences and in our writing. It is the Jesus who said that the final judgment is to do with how we treat the hungry, the strangers, the poor, the sick, the imprisoned. It is the Jesus who told of a feast which will be filled not with the great and the important and the successful but with the poor, the crippled, the blind and the lame. He is the one who challenges every generation with moral imperatives and with the invitation to share in his death and resurrection. But we have stopped our ears and closed our eyes, otherwise our eyes would see, our ears would hear, our minds would understand, 'and they would turn to me, says God, and I would heal them'. Somehow the Jesus of the Gospels, and my detailed and long term study of them, ends in my going over the top like this! It also fuels and directs, underpins and motivates the values I carry with me.

At a minimum there are certain things that our moral values must do. They need to fit in with a world in which we are always searching and journeying. They need to be clear and yet accepting and tolerant. They have to stand the fact of our own death and feel right to us in spite of our own mortality. They need to have some passion to see right prevail but to do this in a non-violent way. They have to be compassionate and yet not overwhelmed by the suffering of others. They have to be fed by our inner resourcefulness and by that human mysticism which stamps with authority the common humanity of all people.

14 Resisting evil

I think that I am motivated in my commitment to justice, peace and love as much by my resistance to evil as by any clear recognition of that which is good and true. Some have suggested that our deep outrage at evil is a sign of our belief in God and certainly it is hard to believe that some things and some actions are anything other than damnable.

Of course many of us do bad, harmful, destructive things to one another. In our better moments, we wish that it were other, but it is difficult to see any sign of human growth which is making such damaging actions less likely. Since I am suggesting that human life is best lived in being creative, affirming and building up,

obviously I see and believe that we should try to resist and overcome even relatively minor breakage.

But I am using the phrase 'resist evil' mainly about major events,
though anyone on the receiving end of anger, jealousy, unkindness
or whatever might feel it is no light-weight thing. But I do want to
concentrate on the Holocaust, Hiroshima, terrorism and torture as
four unspeakable evils which have to be faced up to. My knowledge of them is at second hand, though I have spoken with and
listened to people who have had experience of them. When I read
about them or see films about them I feel confronted by horror and
evil on such a scale that only human heroism and resilience offer
any kind of hope. I remember some of these films making as great
an impact upon me as any of the more personal examples that I
have come across. I do not think we have begun to understand the
destructive and ongoing effect of human violence. In our century
millions have been tortured, murdered, bombed, made slaves, put
into concentration camps, destroyed with chemicals, napalm, and
nuclear weapons. We go on as though nothing has happened. We
go on as though we have not inflicted upon ourselves any serious
or long-term damage. But we have damaged ourselves greatly.

People have different understandings of evil. Some time ago I
watched a children's puppet film. The story was that two human-
like young people had to get a fragment which had been split from
the dark crystal of the title back into place before three suns came
into conjunction. In the story there were two groups of parallel
ancients, one set wise and gentle and the other fierce and ugly and
hard. The journey involved many imaginative, amusing and frightening creatures and a variety of adventures. At the end, the two
characters reach the castle where the dark crystal is in place ready
for the suns to come into line. The ancients were hoping that their
evil rule would continue for a thousand years, but the two young
people get the fragment into place in time, though the girl dies in
the effort. At that point the mystics surround the crystal and as the
light of the three suns passes through the crystal and on through
their eyes, they draw the evil ancients back into themselves. As
they become whole, then new brilliant creatures of light emerge.
These are created by the merging of the two sets of ancients. The
two together were whole – a new creation beyond good and evil.
These creatures of light bring the girl back to life and the earth is

given to the two human-like beings for a further thousand years. The crystal beings fused into one and disappeared.

Now I am using this story for two reasons. The reality of good and evil seems so absolute that we seem to need mythologies to even talk about it.

The second reason was that it was a surprising and astonishing ending. To see before your eyes good and evil merge into such dazzling beauty and goodness was quite mind-bending. It was a new possibility. It was a visual breakthrough from what seemed possible.

So if humans are 'to reclaim the earth', if we are to be among those who choose life rather than death, then we have to resist evil.

I clearly remember the first time I saw film about the Holocaust and the camps during the Nazi time. Over the years I have tried to accept some responsibility to read and view what I can about the camps. This is not because I am in any way fascinated by them, in truth I am always sickened and horrified at what I see. But it has seemed right, at least in a small way, to attempt to take the reality of the camps seriously. They run like a vein of evil through the world's history. I have seen some of the original footage and much more that has been dramatized. I have seen here and in Amsterdam a little of the catalogue of fascism.

Because I was born in 1940 and therefore had no knowledge of the Nazi time I think it would still have remained distant for me. But when we came to London in 1976 fascist parties in Britain were re-emerging. They were involved in attacking and harassing black people and to my utter astonishment they eventually, for a short time, became involved in mainline party politics. I well remember the first time I saw a fascist British leader being interviewed on TV for all the world as though he were somehow a respectable politician. Through my work I spoke, wrote, even marched against them. I suppose I just could not credit that Britain, whose war against Nazism had, as I understood it, been a war against such beliefs, could admit them into the arena of legitimate politics. Whatever the analysis of their activity, then or now, I have always seen them as an extension of all that is worst in us, and all that led to the camps. I recall writing a paper for a conference in the summer of 1983. It was called 'Theological Reflections on Racism and Fascism'. I mention it because it was an occasion at which I found myself pushed to find the Christian basis of my opposition to them. In fact my experiential and political opposition had come first.

I have also seen films about Hiroshima and Nagasaki. I understand a little about the arguments about why the bomb was used, I know a little about Japanese atrocities, conventional bombing and what happened at Dresden. I recently saw a caption to an article about the bomb which used, I think, a quotation from an earlier writer. It said something like 'in or about August 1945 something in human character actually died'. The bomb has become a fact of our lives and of our deepest nightmares. The need for it is argued by politicians who believe that only strength can and will deter aggressors. Others, in different ways, argue that we must find a way to get rid of it. Like the Vietnam War, the Civil Rights Movement in America, the bomb, for some, has become the means to political awareness. What sort of people would use it? The terrible answer is that we would be the same sort of people who used it last time. But it is surely an evil to be resisted with all our force and energy.

My third example is terrorism. Some people argue that in the face of extreme repression, or indeed as part of a war, terrorism is a necessary evil. I cannot see that the bombing or shooting of innocent people can be justified. Terrorism uses fear, harassment, brutality, physical force as its weapons. The victims, whatever rights it is said are being sought and whatever the wrongs of the attacked government or faction, are always counted amongst the innocent bystanders. Surely such actions are truly evil.

My fourth example, though political, is in one sense more personal. Torture has been used maybe always. Today it has become widespread and it is serviced by an arms industry which includes British manufacturers. Once, so we were told, people resisted torture because they were brave and good. Now, the other side of brainwashing and drug torture, we are told people are easily broken. And they are broken in countless numbers by every group and power which lives by repression and fear. Organizations which oppose torture frequently give details of methods and of people whose release is sought. They make grim reading. Here again is an evil to be resisted.

I am giving serious examples. People in our society find it difficult to comprehend the devil, or demons, or 'principalities and
powers'. Evil with a capital 'E' seems outdated and we find it easier
to transpose the battle between good and evil into some future 'star
wars' saga. But there have been and are in our world monstrous
evils that are a threat to every search for humanity and community,
and we must do everything we can to resist and oppose them.

15   Suffering and death

I separate my desire to resist evil from my experience of suffering
and death. Though I must say that I have immediate and strong
resistance to them. I know that some people handle the fact of suffering and death much better than I do. I meet people who deal
with their own serious health problems and disabilities in a brave
and forthright way. I confess that I tend to 'rage against the dying
of the light' whether it is the common cold or a friend with cancer.
The experience of suffering and the bereavement which comes
because of other people's deaths is as much part of the raw material
of my life as my understanding that I will die.

There is a great deal involved in all the processes which break
people down and destroy them. The level of our personal anxieties
and dis-ease is very great. We seem to find it hard to be at home in
ourselves and make ourselves at home in the world. I see in people
I meet and work with such a degree of discontent, isolation, alienation, fear even. Sometimes a film can portray such human dislocation quite vividly. Some classical tragedy choruses human troubles.
And within the social sciences and within medical practice people
strive to understand, cure or at least control our pain. Pain that is
self-inflicted. Pain that comes from disease. Pain that comes
through human relationships. One thing is true, you either learn
to deal with such ordinary suffering or it destroys you.

I remember a time in my first job, sitting in my digs on a rainy
day. I used the excuse of having a cold as a way to hide. I recall the
feeling of nothing, the loss of energy and direction, the sense that
I had run into the sand.

No doubt a number of close encounters with suffering shaped
my view. When I was about twenty I worked for a summer in the

sick ward of a large psychiatric hospital. I saw it as part of the practical training which went with some academic work I was doing at the time. It was an astonishing few months. I was expected, though I had no training at all, to give out medicines, do dressings, give injections, as well as the bed changing and cleaning people up routines. There was a man who thought he was a horse who thanked me, when he got better, for feeding him. There was another with sores on his heels which came because he was constantly walking up and down the ward, but he believed people were pouring acid on him. There was the old man who died of a lung disease who used to lie there with a cigarette in one hand and his oxygen mask in the other. I remember treating gangrene, taking the bandage off a man who had cut his throat, learning what GPI meant. I remember taking left-over food so that I had time to get away and catch the bus home on my day off. I know I was wonderfully unskilled as when a man tried to kill himself by diving through a window. The staff nurse shouted at me because not only, in my haste, did I bring a sterile dressing in my hand, but I also ran down the ward. Of course all this was to do with other people's pain, and, as with the sight of blood, it is my own that upsets me even more.

And yet people can have too much suffering and pain. I experience these both at the very personal level of what has happened to me and to people very close to me. My own personal approach is that the only thing that is good or ennobling about pain is when it stops. Always I experience it as something to be resisted, overcome, fought against. I feel that I am getting up off the floor after I have been knocked down. But I am aware of some grasp of the history of human suffering which is marked by plagues, by the 'flu epidemic after the First World War, by cancer and now by AIDS. Of course I am delighted when we humans find ways to combat disease and cure people. But it is a relentless fight on our complex planet.

One of the things that brings all this home to me very strongly is the TV news. In a way, in the West, it has become a catalogue of disaster. I used to think of the news as 'the' News. Now I experience it in this way. If any system wanted its people to feel either cynical or powerless they could not do it more effectively than the diet of fashioned disaster we call the News. To take it seriously would be to risk madness. To take it as normal is to deaden sensitivity. It is as though we were living in a village and several times a day a traveller stopped off and told everyone about the disasters and sufferings of the world. TV magnifies this, it scoops up and deposits bad news, like decaying maggot-infested slops, at our meal tables. And we wonder why we have indigestion! I know I take the TV too seriously but just as it is a window to so much that is brilliant and life-affirming so I find the News bulletins (and I mean the News specifically) a concentrate of our suffering.

And yet we go on. When I was in Wales as a young minister of religion I used to do quite a lot of funerals. The Welsh tradition then, and still today, was to make the funeral emotional, cathartic and grieving, and then have a good meal together afterwards. Looking back I suspect I saw too many people in their coffins, too much grief, too many tragedies, from the death of children, to road accidents, to murder, to normal lingering deaths. Too much for anyone, maybe, and certainly too much for someone who was simply coping from his own personal resources rather than from any learnt professional ones. But in the years since, when I have known about death through people close to me as well as through my work, I have come to respect the Welsh attempt to have a process of bereavement. In East London, though I have done few of them, funerals are quick, fifteen minute affairs for strangers.

So this is part of the very raw material of my life. It has been a way through which I have been able to get to the other side of my own death and then come back to the business of living it.

When our children were very small I was wakened in the night by their intense and unusual crying. I raced into the room so quickly that I forgot my glasses. There they were standing together on one bed screaming and pointing to the orange rug on which I was standing. I found the dead goldfish with my foot before I understood what they were saying. And then out of this hilarious moment an extraordinary thing happened. Within a matter of minutes they went through all the different stages of grieving that I had learnt to recognize in counselling – shock, anger, depression, disbelief, acceptance. Then it was decided that, since after all Dad was a minister, I should have the honour of doing a funeral at the bottom of the garden, in the snow.

Our resilience, and the humour which is part of that resilience, is astonishing. We hold within ourselves the sense that we are going to die and the sense of being wholly alive in a very real and substantial way. A favourite TV programme, I will not take the easy way out and say of our children, had the line 'Fame, I'm going to live for ever'. There is something bravely death-defying in us. And for so many people there are resources of humanity and caring which enable them to die with self-respect and dignity.

As for what happens after death, I cannot believe that there is nothing for us beyond death. I hope that there will be for me and for us and for humans good things, but we do not know.

Some time ago I was on the Underground. A woman ran past me on the platform and flung herself onto the train through the closing doors. She was struck by the doors but she squeezed through leaving her bag trapped. The platform guard signalled for the doors to be re-opened so as to free her. As the train moved off this young, Chinese or Japanese, woman looked out through the glass door. It was a slow motion event of potential danger. It was an accident in the making. But it did not happen, so we all relaxed and carried on with our lives.

I cannot help but feel that, as humans, we could do much better to cope with our human suffering and the fact of death. We have to help each other live with care and compassion. We have to help each other live both with a strong desire to overcome unnecessary suffering and with an acceptance of death as part of human reality.

16 Living

So these are some of the raw materials, as I call them, which make up my life. They are the things I come back to again and again. I am aware of three elements which run through them and which are in fact raw materials in themselves.

The first is that we have to admit, I have to admit, that there is an enormous puzzle at the centre of life. It is extraordinary to try to place our doubts and uncertainties alongside the sheer otherness of the world we inhabit. At times I get a peculiar and particular sense that in spite of all the questions there is a givenness which is satisfying and yet demanding. So whilst we are in some deep senses puzzled to know what it is all about we are faced with a humanity which is rich and dazzling. We cannot ignore it. We cannot avoid it. We can idealize it or fantasize about it or put ourselves at risk within it. But it is there. And part of what is there is our lack of understanding and our sheer encyclopaedic ignorance.

Yet, at the same time there is so much that happens to me, and that I see happening to other people, which is to do with wholeness. We have experiences which lead us to believe that, in spite of all that divides and breaks down, diminishes and tears apart, there is a deep sense in which people and our world are shot through with meaning and significance. There are times of discovery, insight, excitement, ordinary ecstasy, which are so powerful and so undeniable that they convince us of the oneness of the world. Sometimes we find out, if we are fortunate, that the most ordinary of human needs, as well as our deeper needs for fulfilment and human love, let alone our peak experiences are all, though fragile, dense with meaning.

And through it all, and perhaps most striking of all in our time and place, is the constant experience of change. We can be sure that we shall have to adjust to and accept changes just as certainly as we have in the past. We acclimatize and adapt or we die.

But all these raw materials, as well as the facts of the puzzle, wholeness and change, are all rooted in our lives. Although I am able to put time and energy aside to write this, in fact my life and living go on. Moreover they dictate the rest.

17   Some more stones to mark the way

I arrived after my introduction at four things which are important and precious to me: being life-affirming, seeking to be at home in myself and in the world, pursuing truth and authenticity, and struggling for justice, peace and the integrity of creation on the basis of our common and interdependent humanity. Now I have shown something of the personal experiences and raw materials of my life, let me, to use the image I used before, gather and place some more stones to mark the way.

Listing them is important but even more important is the crucial and formative experience of going through doorways into pluralism. I do not think that I can over-emphasize what this has done to me and for me. It is not, as some would expect, that it has given me an understanding of the relativism of life which has made me either negatively cynical or uncommitted. Rather I have seen the variety, diversity and richness of life and this has strengthened my sense of our common humanity. So we need to welcome pluralism as showing diversity within this common humanity.

The ordinariness of life may seem a strange thing to emphasize. But if I look at what I spend most of my life actually doing and what I use up most of my time on I know that so much of it is ordinary. There is sleep, the routine to do with myself and our family, running the house and bringing up children. Only my work takes me into another situation. I imagine the same is true for many other people. I understand that do-it-yourself house maintenance, gardening, fishing, watching TV, cars, sport, holidays feature high on any list of activities. These rightly or wrongly feel as if they happen outside any ideological sense. They happen, to put it the other way round, from within a framework of assumptions which do not need or warrant criticism. So the ordinary features of our living are to be seen not simply as something whose sense we understand but as amongst the direct and solid experiences of our lives. This is why the word leisure is politically such a tricky word because it suggests that somehow all these things we do are in a safe, shut apart from work, non-ideological world. But they are not. The ordinary things of our lives are it! So we have to value the ordinary things of our lives.

To say that people are important sounds stupid because for most of us there is no escape from other people. They crash into us, impinge on our lives, get behind our guard, help us, support us, flow with us along the streets. But in fact I am pointing to the importance of people and to their worth. Somehow we see in people's worth not only the crucialness of their own identity but also their place within communities. We see that people are most fully human when they achieve some dynamic tension between their own individuality and community. At best neither dominate but both survive and are fulfilled. Two of the ways of achieving this I am sure are to do with learning to stand in other people's shoes and by learning to listen to other people. So I am concerned to assert the worth of people. If that sounds tame or weak, ask all those millions who are treated by the powerful of our world as worthless and find themselves rubbished and on the world's scrapheaps.

I have found it really important to discover that the personal aspects of my life and the political aspects of my life are inseparable. It is, as I recall an African writing, a very Western heresy to believe that we can split apart the private and the public, the personal and the communal, the religious and the political. In fact, however described, they are indeed twins, with their own identities but closely linked together. I think we must see the two-edgedness of our personal and political lives.

The fact of belonging to the Christian church, especially at a local level and with groups of Christians, I count among the real things of my life. Within that my obsession with the Jesus of the Gospels remains firmly in place. My study of them and my learning about them with other Christians has been and is a constant influence. Whatever else belonging to the church means, the Gospels of Jesus are a major reference point, a catalyst, an energizer. I find belonging to the church is at its sharpest in relation to the Jesus of the Gospels.

In terms of conflict and hostility the question of whether or not we can live with and tolerate each other's alternative ways of living and believing is crucial. History and the world today is littered with wars caused by a battle for people's minds and beliefs. This naturally encompasses their cultures, social stratification and possessions. It is of crucial importance for the future of our world for us to find how to live with difference. And we have to discover how to make the distinction between living and accepting differences and challenging that which is unjust and a threat to peace. It is always easiest to see what is unfair or violent in other people's cultures and groups. It is always hardest to perceive what is wrong, and fundamentally wrong, within our own. So, without losing sight of justice and peace, and without being unrealistic about the level of conflict which is likely between people and groups, we have to learn to live with other alternatives.

Whatever our understanding of work and leisure, and of their importance in our lives, most of us use work as a means of getting money to survive and live. And in our society, I would say increasingly, only money is of use to get most things. Even those who have a job which they regard as a vocation also see their jobs as a means to live. Those without work understand, better than most, what this is all about. As I look at our world, whatever political analysis we make of social stratification, power and the distribution of the world's resources, it seems to me that the gap between the rich and the poor is, on a major scale, a constant threat to social and global stability, let alone to prosperity and development. So we must use money and work for the common good and not for the benefits of the few whoever they are.

Our positive understanding and experience of gender, sexuality and sex is crucial if we are to survive and be fulfilled. A positive enjoyment of sex has to be worked out in terms of our relationships with and valuing of other people. What we are to guard against is sex which either uses other people or is violent to other people. Otherwise I see enjoying sex as an experience freed through contraception from the constraints of producing children.

Having the opportunity to be creative, whether through writing, drawing or through other people's creativity in films or art is surely a crucial part of our development. We have to work at it whether we do it through cooking, gardening, model-making, embroidery, knitting, making clothes, carpentry, pigeon fancying or however. We must not allow other people, on the basis of their culture or class, to determine what is creative for us. We must not be de-skilled or discouraged. We must be as creative as we can and use the pleasure and satisfaction that comes from it.

Living on frontiers makes inner space especially precious. We can find it and explore it from many different disciplines, methods and techniques. It comes also through a whole range of life's experiences and is present in all the peak experiences of our life. Without denying the achievements or skills of those who have become experts we should not allow anyone to mystify us. We should not allow anyone to prevent us making these journeys on our own terms and in our own ways. It is not to be separated from the rest of our living but certainly many people attest that they find their way best through guidance from others and when they adopt a disciplined approach. I think that most of us have hardly begun to journey into inner space. To borrow an image from a novelist I have read many times, we still drive with the handbrake on and wonder why we do not experience life all the time with the intensity that comes to us occasionally.

Where you are certainly shapes what you are in East London. The examples and the description express this in very personal terms. The truth is that we are changed and formed by how and where we live. This is true for everyone but in the inner city, where people are often stretched to their limits, this understanding seems undeniable and closer to the surface. We have to recognize the impact of the place where we live and see how it shapes our perceptions and our judgments.

All people and groups have moral values whether or not they call them moral values. The question is why we have the ones we have and how we validate them. Or is it simply that the moral values of the most powerful rule? I see moral values as having to do with being life-affirming, and all else I am listing and summarizing here. In applying them and examining them, whether in relation to racial justice, war and the teaching of Jesus, or in terms of government policies, apartheid, a quarrel with the person next door, or how you live within your own family, we press them into action in a world of compromise, conflict and violence. But it is there they have to work. We have to apply our moral values in this real world.

This is even more true and more difficult when it comes to resisting evil. How to resist evil in a non-violent way seems to me to be the hardest question. Why humans find it necessary to go on killing each other and destroying each other in such large numbers I do not know. That anyone should try to stop someone else being evil and destructive is obvious but to develop the skills and the controls which can make this possible without resorting to violence is so far well beyond us. Resisting evil is rarely straightforward, not least because people disagree, to put it mildly, about who is doing the evil and who is doing the good. But, to return to my examples, the holocaust, the bomb, terrorism and torture seem wholly evil and to be resisted.

Suffering and death threaten to destroy, break down and diminish us. Our experience of them is strongly negative. Yet we go on often with courage and dignity. Indeed we know people and hear of people who, in spite of suffering and the closeness of death, are an inspired example of what it means to be a human being. Some people would express this differently, I know, but I can just about handle suffering and death by angrily accepting them.

Through all this living there remains an enormous puzzle as to what it all means and in what way any of it makes sense. It is hard to answer the question from within the terms of our humanity and yet we cannot give answers which go beyond our experience. But there is also the contradictory experience that sometimes our lives do feel remarkably substantial and we have an attractive and compelling sense of wholeness. Above all we experience a sense of change: we see significant changes taking place in us and around us and so we know that we are in some kind of process and on some sort of journey.

A number of things seem very clear to me at this point and I want to say them now, and before I summarize this even more sharply. I see in what I am attempting the importance of adventuring rather than clinging to what is past or safe for their own sakes. I see the worth of and need for a critical loyalty which is fuelled more by nonconformity and dissent than by convention. I see the need in what I am struggling to express to break free from all that threatens to immerse, submerge, absorb, dominate. I want to show what seems to me to be true rather than simply describe it. I want to get at the truth. I want to make such sense as I can regardless of incompleteness or inconsistency or inadequacy. I want above all to find some ways through to sharing what is important and precious to me in a way that I can accept on its own terms as well as recognize as being Christian.

So let me try, before moving on to the further step of Christian critical reflection, to summarize and put out the stones I have gathered to mark the way. I have been describing a way of living which is important and precious to me and which I have found within my personal experiences and the raw materials of my life.

This way of living and these life-values mean:

Being . . . . . . life-affirming.
Seeking . . . . . to be at home in myself and our world.
Pursuing . . . . . truth and authenticity.
Struggling . . . . for justice, peace and the integrity of creation on the basis of our common and interdependent humanity.
Welcoming . . . . pluralism and diversity.
Valuing . . . . . the ordinary things of our lives.

Asserting . . . . . the worth of people as individuals and in community.

Seeing . . . . the two-edgedness of our personal and political life.

Belonging . . . . . to the church and the Jesus of the Gospels.

Being open . . . . . to other alternatives.

Using . . . . money and work for the common good.

Enjoying . . . . . . sex without using people.

Being . . . . creative in a spontaneous and self-transcendent way.

Journeying . . . . . into inner space in search of autonomy and self-realization.

Recognizing . . . . the impact of the place we live.

Applying . . . . . moral values in situations of compromise, conflict and violence.

Resisting . . . . . . evil, both personal and social evil.

Angrily accepting . . suffering and death.

Tripping over . . . the puzzle, wholeness and change of life.

PART TWO

A Step of Critical Reflection

1 Understanding and translating

So far, so good. By starting from my personal experiences and the raw materials of my life I have arrived at a statement of my life values: those things which are important and precious to me.

Now I want, from this perspective, to show how these life-values fit into my faith as a Christian. I am aware that other Christians proceed in a different direction or start from another place.

I need to reflect on three experiences.

The first one is negative in that I have to try quite hard in order to fit my experiences and raw materials into the theology and sub-culture of our church. To succeed in understanding I have to engage in a process of translation. More positively, I have learnt and shared with other Christians, at a local level, in critical reflection and have found the experience confirming.

The fundamental insight in all this has been doing theology in context.

The usual way of learning about the Christian faith, or indeed about any faith or way of life, is by joining in. The traditional and unavoidable way of finding out what is on offer is to become part of the church and there find out about the life and teaching of Christian people. That is to say we are invited to join in according to the Christian ground rules and the Christian life with its language, mythology, symbols, rituals, festivals, practices, culture.

To give a very different example. I remember when I came to London at first, a friend stood with me in Piccadilly Circus and described something of what was happening around us. He described his own work in the city centre with all its complexities and problems. He asked me what I thought we as Christians and as the church could and should do. Out of my sense of shock at all I had seen and heard I said, 'Well, maybe all we can do is join in.'

And, for many people, this is how it is with the church. We join in, take it, if I may put it like this, on its own terms and do the best we can to make of it what we can and, more importantly, to make out of it what we can of a personal faith.

Of course the truth is that the Christian church and its teaching and life are not one thing but many. In practice people have to choose which part of this family of religions they want to belong to. The fact is, as is evidenced in many parts of the world, it is not enough to describe people as Christian and thereby expect to see them all on the same side on any important issue. And if this is true of major public decisions, which at an extreme leads to people who claim to be Christians killing one another, it is also true in the much more ordinary sense that Christians find it extremely difficult to feel at home in anything other than their own particular type of worship and church life.

So we have to make a personal choice from within many options. And yet all of them have one thing in common. It is that they invite us to join in and belong on their terms.

In working on this section I decided to read a thesis I wrote almost twenty years ago. I found it strange to find that so much material, that had once obviously mattered to me, had completely fallen into disuse. What I had written about was almost entirely made up of other people's ideas and books about the Bible, the New Testament and Christian ethics. It hardly touched ordinary living and experience at all.

I also looked back at some books on theology which give an overview and summary of the range of the subject. They are wholly written from within the community of faith and from inside the received traditions.

Sometimes when I go into a Christian bookshop I really feel trapped. This happens especially in academic bookshops when I realize how out of date I am. It also happens in bookshops which are not of my particular brand of being a Christian, where of course I find it difficult, in practice, to be tolerant of so much that is on the shelves. But in both cases the thing I experience most is the sense of leaving outside the things that are important and precious to me.

One of the problems of being a minister of religion is that most of the time you lead worship and so are not on the receiving end. When I do go to worship in someone else's church I often find it disquieting.

So what am I saying? I am saying that as a student, in the teaching of the church, in Christian bookshops, in church worship, I find a great deal which does not feel to be part of my experiences and raw materials. It feels beyond me, external, foreign, separate, belonging to other people. There is some serious dislocation and dysfunction between what is important and precious to me in my life and what I am invited to join by the Christian faith.

Too often the Christian faith does not sufficiently offer sense and meaning to the life we live, it invites us to join in learning a new language and a new sub-culture. At worst we shall always be struggling to translate from the Christian view to our personal experiences. At best we shall become so fluent in the Christian language and world-view that, once we are in that world, mode, language, we shall be in danger of getting out of touch with anyone else who is outside.

This is what I mean by saying I have to engage in a process of translation.

2 Learning and sharing

Let me look at how I have been doing my Christian critical reflection over the past decade or so. What I have been doing has several parts to it.

First of all I have been wrestling with my own personal faith. I have seen this experience, writing, and reflection as what some people traditionally describe as prayer and study.

Secondly I have shared all this with people close to me and I have tried hard to listen to what has been happening to them. This, of course, has especially included my family but it has also included quite a number of friends with whom I have talked, argued, shared, disagreed, celebrated. I have learned from their attempts at self-expression and self-discovery. Although much of this has been informal and even casual, it has nonetheless been a way of testing and developing what I believe in myself.

Thirdly I have from time to time joined with small groups of Christians who have chosen to address these issues of how you work out faith starting from the place in which you find yourself. Over the years I have met with groups in East London and also in other cities, and always we have had a desire to learn from other people who are doing theology from their context. Always we have been interested in listening to Christians from Third World countries and from situations where the church is taking sides with the poor and oppressed. We have tried, given the example of Christians in different parts of the world, to look at what is happening to us and to see if we can discover an equivalent contextual theology for ourselves. This has meant looking at our own situation at least as seriously as we look at situations described by others in books. Often these groups have been frustrating and short-lived. Sometimes they have been abrasive and divisive. But they have been an extremely important way of learning about our faith in this time and place.

Fourthly I have belonged for fifteen years to our small Christian church in East London. Without being romantic about it or making foolish claims about it, the church tried to put its hands to two things. We tried to find ways within Sunday worship which would allow people to participate on their own terms. This included Bible study which was sometimes genuinely an expression of people's lives. We also tried to develop a community work programme, which whilst informal and modest in style, used our very good premises as space in which people could meet. Individuals and groups could meet in safety. They could do their own activities. They could if they chose use our staff for advice, counselling and Christian contact. I must say that I am always suspicious of Christians who only belong to self-selected groups and do not root themselves with an ordinary local congregation. Our action and first reflection take place within the faith of a Christian community and I would say we need each other if we are to find our way through.

Finally, for fifteen years or more, I have focussed some of my work on the issue of racial justice. We chose to live in a multi-racial neighbourhood. This has led me, even more than working on the issues of the inner city in general, into insights and ways of seeing society which have quite changed me. Putting it boldly, and without claiming too much for myself as a white person, I have come to see the dangers of seeing the world from a European, English or white perspective only. I have come to see the great evil which, in shorthand, is referred to as racism and which includes that prejudice and power which systematically disadvantage people and communities who belong to the ethnic minorities in British society. The point is that because I have been privileged to live, work and worship with black colleagues and friends I have had the opportunity to see something of what it means to be on the receiving end of such racism. I have also been able to see some of the positives and strengths that the black, Asian and all ethnic minority communities bring to our society.

So I am aware that in these five overlapping ways I have been involved in Christian critical reflection. The thing they have in common is that they all do theology, reflect critically, from the context of what is happening to us as individuals and communities.

3 Doing theology in context

There is no doubt that at this point I really would like to describe and get into the books and people whose contextual theology and action have so helped and impressed me over the years. I think of people I have met and books I have read which have changed me, challenged me, pushed me to act differently. Such people have come from the Third World, from black American or South African theology, from the liberation theology of Latin America, from political theology, from feminist theology, from the cultural theology of Africa or South East Asia. I remember them with gratitude and have learnt so much from them.

But if such people and books teach anything it is that we must all begin from our own experiences and context. And so I must stick with it. I must not be diverted because in comparison with other situations what I am saying feels not dramatic enough or activist enough or analytical enough. I must take a further step of critical reflection but I can only do it from my time and place, the people with whom I live, the Christians with whom I cluster, and those people who have neither justice or peace with whom I take sides.

So I have no doubt for myself, or in fact for Christians in inner city and multi-ethnic, multi-faith, multi-language, multi-cultural neighbourhoods and communities, that I am approaching this task the right way round. This method of taking this further step of critical reflection is described by one writer as 'a second step of critical reflection which follows after the praxis of faith'. Let me say what this means both from my own experience and, as I understand them, from the perception of those contextual writers who are wrestling with issues of justice and peace among the oppressed and dispossessed of the world.

I want to focus on five aspects of this process and method. I believe they will show up clearly the relation between those things which I have described as important and precious to me and the Christian critical reflection which I am as a Christian obliged to do.

First and above all we have to take the experiences, situation and context seriously. We have to stay within them and interpret them on their own terms. In this we have to recognize the extent of our own self-interest. All humans want to survive and if possible be fulfilled. And, the more we have, the more most of us want. But we have to set against this our experience and perception of other people's needs and not just the people who are like us, our kith and kin, but all the people of whom we are a part in society, and in fact throughout the world. This concern for our common humanity and our interdependence is the basis for compassion and for taking sides especially with those who are in need, the poor, disadvantaged, those who are denied their legal human rights, those who are dominated and oppressed.

Two questions keep troubling me. Can we see clearly, can we see what is significant, exceptional, precious and important? I believe we can, especially from within a community of people and especially if we strive to look from the vantage point of other people. We are back to standing in other people's shoes and listening to what people are saying. The second question overlaps. It is, who pays the price, what is the cost, who is doing the suffering? So much of our life is about conflict, compromise, violence. That is how it is. But to take the context seriously means taking the whole and long term situation seriously. A test of this is that whenever our own self-interest is most easily and generously satisfied we should look around to see who in fact is picking up the price tag and whether or not our actions cause damage, hurt and suffering to other people.

Secondly, as a Christian I belong within the community of faith. The task of critical reflection does mean checking my own personal faith and statement of what is important and precious against that of other Christians. I recognize again how differently different parts of the church do this. For some it means accepting the teaching and authority of the church and seeking to get the church's validation. For others it means conforming within a Christian language, practice, experience. For others it means being critical of the church. My experience has been that by belonging to a particular local Christian congregation and by working with some other groups of Christians I have found worship, fellowship, study, evangelism, service and political action which has strengthened and run in harness with all that has been happening to me personally. I am conscious because of this Christian experience of several factors which I need to bring to bear on what I am writing and in this critical reflection.

Let me list them.

– Other Christians with whom I meet have a right to be critical of my description of our context.

– I am strengthened by their study and action and I need allies in order to keep going.

– I see the example in action, in the lives and witness of other people, and this constantly inspires and challenges me.

– I see, especially in the church's work with those who are in need and who pay the price in their suffering of decisions they have not made, a constant perspective and extension of my own life. I have not chosen to become one of the poor and needy but I have chosen to identify with them and take sides with them.

– I am conscious, from other Christians, that I miss out certain important emphases in the Christian faith.

– I am glad that with other Christians I have the opportunity to keep on studying the Gospels of Jesus.

– I am helped by the fact that I belong with other Christians for whom emotion and passion, caring and love, count as much, at least, as thinking and words.

– I am aware that the community of Christians with whom I have worked and to which I belong copes with my doubts rather than attacks me because of them.

Thirdly, it is necessary to bring to this critical reflection and analysis the very best insights and wisdom that we can lay our hands on. We have to look at other disciplines and ideologies from around our plural society and see what there is in them which we can use to sharpen the tools of our own critical reflection. This raises for me two important issues. The first is how we deal with certainty and doubt when there are so many options and so much that at best appears relative. The second is how we discern the serious omissions we make, whether we choose to seek to correct them or we simply choose to live with them. It sounds far too patronizing and far too simple to divide the world into two kinds of people. But, whatever the explanation, it does seem to be the case that some of us choose to operate with a very authoritarian and hard-edged model of life and others adopt a more adventuring and flexible model. It only takes a moment's thought of people we know to see how people of these different personalities and temperaments clash even if they share the same ideology. I suspect that our certainties and doubts are at least as much to do with who we are as with what we claim to believe. As for omissions, I do not of course care about omitting things with which I disagree! So there is not a great deal in what I have to write about the importance of making a lot of money at any cost (to other people), or how to become a torturer in three easy lessons, or how to be a successful drug dealer. The omissions which matter come from realizing the limits of my own experience and recognizing in the experience of others that which I value.

Let me mention four as examples:

– There are people whose lives display a level or depth of fulfilment which has been gained through a direct service to people. Their compassion and the daily, detailed, self-giving routine of their lives impress me greatly.

– There are people in extreme situations who have taken sides with the poor, who as Christians have adopted a Marxist analysis

of social class and social stratification and the power which under-
lies such a system, and it has become a viable tool for them. In
Britain, in our free society, it is very hard to discuss the insights of
Marxian analysis and their contribution to understanding without
being dismissed and marginalized. And it will get harder.

– There are people who face up to some of the hard things of
life in a very impressive way. People who face illness. People who
handle the dark side of life. People who cope with betrayal, guilt
and embarrassment in quite a different way.

– There are Christians, and people of other faiths, who witness
to an experience of God and a process of grace which sounds and
feels different from what is happening to me. Some have a deep and
almost intuitive faith. Others witness to changed lives. Others take
experiences of God almost for granted. Others, at their best, share
their certainty and graciousness.

Fourthly, it is vital to read and study the Christian Bible and to
do this with other people. Many different groups of people have
engaged in doing theology in a contextual way. Alongside their
approach and within their experience has been shared study of the
scriptures. Some Christians begin from the scriptures and indeed
literalists will not depart from them. My experience personally and
within the local church is that the experiences of our lives can become a way into understanding the Christian Bible. We take
account of the Jewish books and the letters and writings of the
early church. But for me the Gospels of Jesus are a source of constant challenge and inspiration. Of course we have to use all the
critical acumen that we can muster, we have also to read them as
four accounts of the life, death and witnessed resurrection of the
man Jesus of Nazareth who was named by his followers as the
Christ. But we have also to bring to them our own real experiences.
I have found that the Jesus of the Gospels confirms, lights up,
challenges, makes fun of, runs a coach and four through, puts
spirit into, puts flesh on, kills off, brings to life again.

There are as many pictures of Jesus as once there were lives of
Jesus and all tell at least as much about the writer as about Jesus.
But we have both to strive to get at the truth and to live with the
reality that people understand and to interpret the Gospels differently and most certainly in different languages.

A poster I often see says 'Jesus is alive, until you meet him, you just haven't lived.' For some Christians this means what it says and moreover they believe they are communicating to other people through a public poster. To me it is so coded that I cannot imagine that anyone outside the church will understand, and moreover I do not think what it says is true. Jesus is not in the normal use of the word, alive, he is risen. Only the people including the disciples met Jesus and the Gospels themselves speak of the blessing that comes to those who have faith but have not seen him. To say that we haven't lived is real Coca-cola advertizing! But it is not the real thing. I use this poster example because one of the realities of our faith in Jesus and our use of the Gospels is that we, as it were, end up at one another's throats. People use the Gospels in different ways and maybe the best we can do is to be as tolerant as we can towards other people's interpretations and as rigorous as we can with our own.

Another way of getting at the faith about Jesus through the scriptures and the Gospels in particular is to attempt some credal statement. A number of years ago I was involved with a small group in the Methodist Church who were asked to produce a simple leaflet describing Christian faith. Maybe I am the only person who still has a copy. It says:

It takes all sorts – all sorts of people – all sorts of Christians – but all Christians

. . . Look to Jesus as their founder.
   They believe that Jesus is special for everyone, because of who he is, because of the life he lived, the things he taught, the way he died, and because he burst into life again.
   They believe he shows God's love has no limits: he makes sense of life and death, and shows us how to live.
   He can be all this 'for everyone'.

. . . Live as followers of Jesus.
   They try to be loving and human and forgiving – with his help – in the whole of their lives: with their families and friends, at work, at leisure, in their neighbourhood.
   They want to change the world into a place of love, peace and justice, 'with everyone'.

. . . Belong to the world church.
They meet together in churches, homes, factories, schools.
They share their lives as a community and as friends, they worship, pray and learn from the Bible and other Christian teaching.
They bring their children into the life of the church, they share in activities which reach out in words of witness and deeds of service 'to everyone'.

I think it is very normal and ordinary to want to try to express our faith in an almost credal sense. I am not talking now about authority but rather about a very human desire to sum up and spell out in a simple, memorable, usable way what your faith is all about. These words were one such attempt.

It is also important to attempt your own personal statement about Jesus that you have found and worked out through studying the Gospels over the years. Here is one of my attempts. Its starting point was an Indonesian drawing of Christ at Easter making a jump from the cross. I used it as a meditation for Easter for our work at the Bow Mission.

We offer this meditation, 'The jump from the cross', for Easter in the context of all our work at Bow. At times we are acutely aware of human suffering and need: at times we share in joy with those who celebrate life.

You say, 'Tell us about it then, in ordinary words, so that we can understand: be down to earth, put away your books, your visions and your dreams, talk of money, bread and power.'

Well, listen to this then. Many of you will have watched the story of Moses on TV. It is the story of a people, a people escaping from slavery – enduring hardships – gaining their heart's desire in a promised land. It is a story which has been told and sung, shaped and reshaped, through many generations. It is a story of a people passing through a sea to freedom.

Like many of the great stories of human history it has a power which makes it alive and relevant whenever it is told. When we hear it, we are amazed and we thrill at its audacity. People say of it, 'All we can do is to tell the story.'

We Christians have a story. It is one of these very old, very potent stories. It is also to do with breaking through barriers, being freed from prisons, overcoming dominations. It is to do with the time 'the blind can see, the lame walk, the lepers are made clean, the dead are raised to life, and the good news is preached to the poor' (Matt. 11.5). Our story is a mind-bender and a life-shaper.

What could be more extraordinary than frozen earth out of which crops grow, or cells dividing and forming human beings, or a concrete polluted city becoming habitable? What could be more extraordinary than that, in a place of flyovers and flats, dereliction and loneliness, there can be healing, community and togetherness?

Our story is about Jesus who made 'the jump from the cross'. Jesus' life and death split open the whole of human history – – his importance is born again in each generation. We see in his suffering how at times our whole world rears up against us and flattens us leaving us powerless. We see in his works of forgiveness and in the ongoing energy of his life our cry for life – the cry of a newborn baby at the moment of death. He leaps clean through into new territories and new worlds.

You say, 'Tell it in ordinary words so that we can understand: be down to earth – put away your books, your visions and your dreams. Talk of money, bread and power.'

At Eastertime people tell the story of Jesus. It is a story which tells us how Jesus who died on the cross 'burst into life again'. It is a story which tells us how Jesus who died on the cross 'jumps from the cross towards the new day which breaks on the horizon'. What do you make of it?

. . . Talk of money . . . Here is a man who says, 'Go and sell all you have and give the money to the poor.'

. . . Talk of bread . . . Here is a man who says, 'Take it, this is my body.'

. . . Talk of power . . . Here is a man who says, 'Whoever wants to be first must place himself last of all and be the servant of all.'

What do you make of it? What can we do with it? How can we understand it in our day?

When we do Bible study together, within worship or in some small group, we have discovered that if we do not tell people what we think the story or saying means, but if we narrate it to them (perhaps with the help of some simple drawings and ideas on a worksheet) people are more than able to put into and get out of the story or saying significant things. We have often found it best to pose one or two very direct questions to get the small groups going. We have found that once they get started there is excitement, personal involvement and new insights to be shared with the whole congregation.

There is no doubt that the Gospels of Jesus provide a way through. What has mattered to me over the years is the way they have been a stimulus to faith and action. As we have studied them as critically as we are able, as we recognize the limits of our own scholarship as a group of Christians, as we bring to them our own lives and insights so they have been for me, and I think for us as a church, life-giving and life-affirming texts and experiences.

PART THREE

How?

I began with what is important and precious to me and came at it through our children, writing, blocks, until I set out four statements as stones to mark the way. Then (in Part One) I tried to describe the main personal experiences and raw materials of my life in an order and way which feels to confirm what I am showing. I summarized the life-values and listed them as an active way of living. Then (in Part Two) I have taken a step of critical reflection as a Christian. I have in writing this very personal account but not in other things that I have tried to do resisted understanding and translating the Christian faith and somehow matching it up to what I have experienced. Rather I have tried to take a step which above all else takes my situation and context seriously and which looks for criticism, comment, verification from those Christians with whom I live, work and worship.

I said at the outset that the main point of what I am writing is to show something of my personal life as a Christian. In traditional terms I am trying to give an account of my spirituality and of the personal and political life which goes with it.

For many years when I wrestled with these issues, I used the term 'End-words' to describe this way of living. I saw this word as including visions and concrete reality, middle axioms and slogans, the individual and the social. I used End-words to mean that words such as justice, peace, love, life-enhancing and the rest are, for me, the words at the end of a process. I also used the term in the Christian sense that they are words about that Kingdom of God to which Jesus pointed which is both here and now and yet in the future. But having worked at this again I will call this way of living a way of life-values. It is even simpler, it is less excluding, and it strikes straight at my deepest belief and understanding that the

Christian way of life, if it is at all on the right lines and at all derived from the life of the Jesus of the Gospels, is to do with being life-affirming. I hope that these life-values will be recognizably a description, statement and witness to this way of living. I hope it will be especially recognizable to other Christians. It is a way I have found through living. It is a way I see confirmed in the local Christian church. It is a way I find in the Gospels of Jesus as I continue to study them. I believe it is recognizably one way of living rather than another. I believe it is a way of living which is both possible and fulfilling.

So having got so far I want to make one final attempt to describe these life-values and this way of living which comes for me from the interaction between my experiences and the life of the Christian church as it is centred around the Gospels of Jesus. To use traditional language, I am describing what it means to be a disciple and follower of this Christ-like way of life. I am spelling out, having begun with the raw materials of my life, my personal way which combines, as it must, spirituality and politics. But the question I most now want to face is the question how? Given the compromise, conflict, and violence of our world, given the fact that faith has to operate within a plural world, given that there are many uncertainties and doubts, how can I and do I strive to put these life-values into practice?

1 Do it

If my approach has communicated anything at all I expect that people will have noticed that I tend towards being an activist rather than a quietist. This seems to be how I am, and at times I wish I could sit more freely to my life and the world. At times I wish I could cultivate a more detached compassion. But I cannot and do not want to. I have found myself describing the life-values which emerged from my personal experiences in a very active way – being, seeking, pursuing, struggling and so on. And I think that is right. Someone has said that the road to holiness and wholeness leads through action.

Certainly what I have found is that the actions and experiences of my life never go away. The raw materials I have described have nagged away at me and obsessed me over the years. They are the actions which sustain me and without which I feel lost and think I could not survive. They are among the things I reach for when I am most desperate, lonely or despairing. They have the power to make me feel alive again. They are the things which in my best and happiest moments make me creative and fulfilled.

So I believe we have to join in and be committed and get on with it. Living with these life-values is something of an adventure and certainly involves a lot of risk-taking. I would not say I am by temperament among the mountain climbers or pot-holers of this world. Indeed at times I can generate enough nervous anxiety before a simple journey to bring the whole family to its knees or at least to my throat. But in terms of these life-values action means taking risks and being adventurous. It means not settling for conformity too easily, it means trying to get to the root of things, it means taking sides, it means losing, it means being in a minority.

All of us are influenced by the classic and traditional forces of home, state, education, media, religion, culture. But if I have to face the question why anyone should follow the life-values and way of living I am describing, I reach several answers. How can people be persuaded? I believe it is in people's self-interest in the sense that it leads to personal maturity and fulfilment, and because concern for all people is a long-term goal for survival. I believe that, within a plural society and all the relativism of our world, we have to discover moral values which at least most people are prepared to hold in common. Obviously these are subject to culture and obviously they are changing. But unless we have some understanding of trying to develop and sustain a moral way of living which is genuinely one of justice and compassion, then our system risks becoming arbitrary or is hijacked by the most powerful and, often, the most corrupt. Naturally we all like to point to authorities to back up the things we claim are right. Every group, society, culture, religion, has its own internal validation through scriptures, people, institutions. But in addition there is much in the law of the land and much in agreements such as the United Nations Declaration on Human Rights 1948 which is in line with the life-values I am putting forward. Of course for some people the force of persuasion is such that they cannot abide people rejecting their values and so they resort to violence so as to compel them. I think that the great strength of the way I am describing is that it only makes sense as a voluntary but thorough commitment.

There is a lot of talk in our present society about the value of hard men and iron women. It is said that strength, resolution, being threatening, winning is everything. Whether in making the nation wealthy, in our relations with other countries or in dealing with dissatisfactions within our own society, might is right. The weakest to the wall. Adapt to being competitive, ruthless, go-getting or die – or at least sod off! Such a view of people and society operates at great cost to those who are broken by it, excluded from it or exploited by it. It is a way in which others always pay the price and do the suffering, however much compassion has to be frozen within cold hearts and steely eyes.

Of course there are practical difficulties in making these life-values work. It is not easy and it is self-defeating to become trapped into some unachievable perfectionism. But it is crucial to realize that winning is not, in every case, everything. There are times when what matters is to make an attempt to be life-affirming, that what counts is being faithful, that the way forward is to make your witness to what you believe in. There are situations in which you know you cannot win but in which, nonetheless, you choose to act in the way of these life-values. Sometimes you do this because you know that registering what you believe is all that is possible. Sometimes you do it because you know that without your input or action the situation would be even worse. Sometimes it is a matter of protest. Sometimes it is a case of putting down your marker so as to gain allies. In any event there is point and purpose in resisting attitudes, actions and policies which you believe to be wrong. It is neither weak, pointless or defeatist. It is essential that we positively engage with these life-values whenever and wherever we can.

So these life-values are about a very different way. And at this present time in our society they run against the mainstream, against the grain, against the dominant power. In this sense it is very much a way of adventuring and risk. But it is a far greater risk to win the whole world at the cost of our true selves, to use a phrase of Jesus.

There have been vast numbers of books written and even more

arguments have taken place about why people ought to follow one way of life rather than another. I suspect that what actually happens is that in some real and living sense value systems swirl and clash together like so much flood water. And beneath some strong currents tug away to shape, move, change, sweep away, divert the common moral value systems that a particular group or society or nation holds to.

But above all you have to do it: you have to practice. This way of living is about striving to choose love not hatred, peace not war, blessings not curses, justice not injustice, forgiveness not revenge, collaboration not ruthless elitism. As with everything else in life you improve at it if you practice. Of course it is not always achievable, of course it is not possible to succeed in every situation, but what matters is the commitment to the general direction. This is the way to go, so walk in it.

2 Be at home in yourself

One of the bad things that happened to me on this journey was when I found myself through my work so caring about the issues and the lives of other people that I could find no fulfilment or satisfaction in what I and we had. It was a hard and difficult time. It was a time of being out of step and out of harmony for the sake of things I believed in and desperately cared about. I realized eventually how destructive it was and I have learnt from other people that even in extreme situations, and mine was hardly that except within my own head, it is right and important to be at home in yourself.

There have been many serious and different attempts to explain why we humans are as we are and why so many humans deal with life, stress and conflict in such destructive ways. I will not rehearse them here. But it is important to register that our ability to live healthy lives and lives which do not seriously damage other people is very much to do with how we learn to cope with the stresses and threats to our survival. These attack us genetically, biologically from our birth, or some say even before birth, and socially. We all learn, to a greater or lesser extent, a whole battery of defensive skills. But it is disastrous if these, instead of being a means to wholeness and survival, become unhealthy and damaging. We have real problems if we become fixed in a position of defensiveness or stuck in postures of avoidance.

But there are also many attempts to describe what it means to be at home in yourself, what it means to be right and at one with yourself, what it means to realize yourself and be fulfilled. I have found a whole range of concepts helpful. They include autonomy, awareness, intimacy, spontaneity, creativity, humour, self-realization and self-transcendence. They are to be found and worked for in the most ordinary things of life as well as in our most precious peak experiences, say, within loving sex, meditation, listening to music, seeing a sunset, eating a meal with people you love.

Three very different influences come to mind. The Orthodox churches teach that God became man in Jesus so that people could become God. Of course people who believe they are God are extremely dangerous and there are far too many of them around the world! But the idea that humans have within them the possibility of being so much more than we have as yet realized seems to me very attractive. We give far more time and energy to developing weapon systems than we do to helping the people of the world fulfil their potential to be daughters and sons of God.

Another is that the women's movement and feminism have made me realize just how hard it is to be at home in myself as a man unless I come to terms with some of the insights of the women's movement about gender, roles, sexuality and, of course, equality and liberation for women. My growing awareness of the extent of male domination and exploitation of women throughout the world has been matched by my attempt to change what I am, especially towards the women with whom I share my life. This is a major example of the insight that we cannot be wholly at home in ourselves if and when we are, in some major and significant ways, smashing up other people's lives. This requires a genuine conversion, repentance, forgiveness. It involves us in constant reappraisal and constant negotiation.

The final influence at this point comes from Buddhism, which in some ways has more to say than either Jesus or the Christian faith about how to be at home in yourself. It speaks for example of serenity, flow and rightness. I have found over the years that some of the Buddhist ideas of sitting loose to life, the impact of direct insight and experience, the energy released by koan sayings, and the sheer irreverence of Zen, so stimulating. I am eating a very strong and delicious olive as I type this and if I had more sense I would concentrate on the taste and not on the typing.

There are many signs of what it means to be at home in yourself. Let me mention four which seem crucial.

Being at home in yourself is to do with a deep happiness. Jesus spoke of the blessedness and happiness which belongs to those who are doing the deeds of God's Kingdom. There is hardly a simpler word or experience. I am sure that everyone knows the distinction between being happy and not and equally they know when they are making other people unhappy. True happiness is not anchored in prosperity or success. In talking about the needs of the world's poor I remember an Asian friend saying to me, 'No one is really poor till they are dead.' He was in line with others who have spoken of a poverty of spirit which leaves so many empty and hungry. None of us in saying this are, for a single moment, being deflected from the urgent need to feed the world. But all are pointing to the truth that happiness, personal satisfaction and human dignity are capable of sustaining people in extreme and astonishingly difficult circumstances. Being at home in yourself means knowing something of these riches.

It also means coping with and owning those things in yourself which you do not like and which those close to you do not like. There is nothing perfectionist in what I am describing. To be at home means knowing your own faults and weaknesses and trying to deal with them. It means admitting those ordinary human negatives which seem to trouble most of us to a greater or lesser extent. It means trying to handle bad experiences, anger, violence, disloyalty, greed and all the rest. It means both admitting them and working to minimize them. One counselling discipline speaks of our need to discharge bad experiences and to get them out of our system. I think one of our responsibilities, in being at home in ourselves, is knowing when we need help and where to get it from.

In a strange way I suspect it is not possible to be truly at home in yourself without other people. I am sure there are exceptional circumstances but generally we need other people not only to help define us but also to help us be healthy. I see one sign of being at home in the ability to co-operate. I think being collaborative, working in fellowship and solidarity, discovering styles of leadership which are more to do with partnership than with authority, finding new ways of participation, are all crucial. They are in the social and political sense a fundamental corrective to the misuse of power. And for the individual they can provide openings for sensitivity and maturity. What is more, I find such collaboration to be creative and more effective.

My final example of what being at home in yourself means is to do with forgiveness. None of us live very long before we find ourselves in situations where we have to forgive other people or ask their forgiveness. We do not use the word or forgive people formally very often. But maybe we are mistaken in that. Maybe that just as societies need means of expressing forgiveness, when great wrongs occur, and rarely find how to make them, so individuals need a more formal way of forgiving one another. When we do not forgive we carry around with us memories, experiences, emotions, ideas which are capable of spoiling and destroying.

So this is part of it. We have to find ourselves and where we are with other people and be at home there.

3 Be at home in the world

We need to take the world, our planet, seriously. We have to see it as a place of potential joy and blessing for all people.

Two images have stayed with me. One is the photograph of the earth from space. It shows our planet incontrovertibly a sphere – well, almost a sphere. It gives us a sense of the fact that we are in truth part of one world and yet at the same time it places us as a planet within all the unknowns of the galaxies and space.

The other is a projection of the earth's surface which makes a map showing the real surface areas of the continents. It shows up dramatically how such a given thing as a map had in fact been shaped and twisted by a view of the world which literally claimed too much ground space for Europe. This map, showing the north and south in new proportions, makes a telling political comment. Some friends of mine were so fascinated by the new image when they saw it at first that they purposely put it upside down on the wall.

For me being at home in the world means working for several things. It means caring about the planet as such. In recent years more people have come to care about ecology and the environment. I remember in my first weeks at university when every subject I went into spoke of the environment. I did not even know how to spell it. But our reverence for the planet flows from the life-values. It means opposing those things which seek to destroy it and campaigning to stop human misuse of it. Examples include acid rain, lead in petrol, gas leaks and other industrial disasters, destroying the rain forests, misuse of animals and allowing species to become extinct. And of course there is all that is contained in the realities of the Chernobyl nuclear disaster and the Bomb. If we believe with the psalmist that we are to renew the earth, then we work to be at home in it. The fact is that so much is threatened, destroyed, and done for profit that the forces against ecology are very great. But we must persist.

Being at home in the world also applies to other people. I see the pluralism of the world and all our differences not as a necessary cause of violence but as an opportunity for celebration. Whether we are speaking of differences between nations and cultures, between national minorities, between religious faiths, between political ideologies or whatever, conflict often comes not because the systems are in themselves conflicting but because people and groups cannot abide other people and groups living differently. So they seek to convert, steal the land, educate, culturally dominate or even brainwash. But the life-values suggest that it is possible to live with difference. I think we shall only be at home in the world, let alone secure a safe future for our planet, if we do this.

I remember the times I had to speak to rural or suburban churches about inner city work. Often people protested that there was no way they could understand because they could not see for themselves. Many people of course travel around the world and have seen some of the world's people for themselves. But I think it is worth pointing out just how much the world's people are accessible to us now. I do not think it is superficial to say that we learn of people through their foods, clothes, music, drama, art. These are available in many cities, in exhibitions and on

TV. Also, whilst there are serious problems of viewing other peoples from the outside, some of the TV programmes about the peoples of the world are quite stunning. Add to this films made from around the world and you have the beginning of a wide range of experience. If only we will switch on and if only we will look.

Being at home in the world also means learning, as we have to as individuals, about the bad things of our earth. It is certainly true that in addition to all that humans do to spoil the earth there is much in our planet that is inhospitable. For many, many people the odds of survival remain slight: there is too much disease, disaster, starvation and death. Maybe all we can do is to work against such situations. But if we are to feel at home in the world we also need to come to terms with its harshness and complexity. At the centre of all this is an enormous puzzle which raises questions about the origin and destiny of the planet and its species. We cannot wait for scientists to find solutions and answers before we feel at home any more than we can wait for total certainty in our faith. But somehow within all the uncertainties, with all the ever changing insights as to what life itself is and is all about, with all the clashing forces within nature and life, we have to make ourselves at home.

There is a whole range of issues which in one sense are on the edge of what I am describing. Maybe we shall only feel at home when we pull them from the periphery to the centre of our concerns and enquiry. Religion has always been capable of offering poetic, mystical, mythological stories about creation. Whatever science offers as an explanation about how we began there is a deep need for that explanation to contain ideas that we can really understand and work with. In the same way the exploration of space – if we can resist turning it into a celestial war zone – continues to float the possibility of there being intelligent life on other planets. Whether or not there is other life in all the galaxies, what does that mean for us? Some of the stories and science fiction films of our time are not only journeys of adventure but at their best they raise, in modern versions, questions about where the earth fits into the map and meaning of space. Religion has also traditionally offered not just comfort to the bereaved or hope to the dying but a way of seeing life beyond death. It is more than possible to live a wholly affirmative life on earth and believe that death is the end of human existence. I do not see that meaning within life is dependent upon belief in there being life after death. But the religions of the world, in a whole variety and complex of ways, have attempted to offer an emotional as well as a faith answer to the human hope for continuing existence. Most people say that we cannot know, some believe that they do know. All of us, I suspect, have a deep need and desire not only to prolong our own existence but to believe, in some meaningful sense, that what we are does not stop when other people grieve at our death.

So, as with being individuals and living in community, we have to be at home in a world which is never an idealized utopia but always capable of wonder and terror. It is quite literally our home and we have to shape and form our lives so that we are at home here.

4   Affirm life, in spite of all

I really believe that by being life-affirming we are going the right way.

Yet, in almost every case, whether individual or socio-political, it always feels as if there is so much that is preventing and opposing us. We have a very solid and real sense of all that destroys, breaks down and diminishes. And even more we know how often the choices we have to make are not between good or bad but between the lesser of several evils. We know how often we find ourselves in situations of compromise and complexity. As I said earlier, we always join in part way through, and very often, because we did not set the ground rules and because we are in no sense in control, it is impossible to affirm life. So I am making the point as strongly as I can that when we affirm life we are doing it in spite of some strong opposition.

Jesus in the Gospels speaks of the ordinariness of human family love and of the fact that love and being life-affirming should be and is expected to be a normal and natural part of family life. The extent of brokenness and hurt within families only underlines how hard it is, whatever the reasons, to be life-affirming in our society. Our inability to be at home in ourselves and our sense of alienation from others lead to breakdowns within our relationships with people we love and we see the disastrous harvest in divorce, psychiatric illness, child abuse and the rest. Whatever shape our family might take, and there are undoubtedly a growing variety, we are to seek to be life-affirming in them. The skills of negotiation, resolving conflict, practising forgiveness, learning to adapt, being loyal are not sufficiently on any educational agendas. But affirming life within the safest and most demanding of human settings is so important. People have described the family as a prison of love and there is no doubt that in the name of love terrible things happen between partners, between parents and children, and in the name of family unity. It is also true that most of us have our most human and most precious experiences within our families. The need to be life-affirming there is critical if we are to be whole people.

But the point Jesus was making was that he expected his followers to do the extraordinary and love people who did not belong within the circle of love and privilege. All of us know that to be life-affirming when the other person or group is against you or even out to destroy you is agonizingly difficult. To me being life-affirming means not using violence or trying not to be violent. When we are bullied or when hurt is done to us by people we love it is very hard not to retaliate. An eye for an eye is an old saying which is well practised within many cultures and societies. But forgiveness, giving way, making space, seeking to resolve conflict by non-violent means are all part of being life-affirming.

Anyone who drives a car, not least in London or on a motorway, knows that a day hardly goes by without someone else's bad driving endangering you. Setting aside the possibility that the fault is ever mine!, being life-affirming means not hooting at the other car, not cutting back in front of it as he did to you, not shaking your fist at her as she did at you, trying to drive responsibly.

Or to take another example. Sometimes we have to continue in a relationship with a person even though there is considerable antipathy between us. It may be a next-door neighbour, someone at work, someone at church, or even someone making obscene phone calls. Being life-affirming does not mean giving in to what you see as the unreasonableness or hurtfulness of the other person in the quarrel but looking for ways of negotiating a way out of the stalemate. Sometimes it means waiting and doing nothing for a

long time, sometimes it means getting advice and even direct help
from another person, sometimes it means resorting to cool politeness. Sometimes it leads to misjudgments. Sometimes it means
anger, blowing up, getting it out of your system.

To be life-affirming is to be creative, it is to cultivate growth, it
is to construct and build. It means setting people free rather than
enslaving or imprisoning. It means cherishing life rather than
handing out death sentences.

Being life-affirming can be expressed in terms of health and
healing. I remember in the few months that I worked as a student
nurse in a psychiatric hospital that, hard and grim as it was, there
was a very direct sense of the worth of caring for people. It is rather
like feeding a child or helping an elderly person. The demands are
obvious and of course can be overwhelming. But in the action of
nursing itself there is something obviously and totally right.

Everyone wants to be healthy and some people have to work
very hard at surviving their ill health. But one of the things I have
noticed in the work of people who are concerned with all types of
healing is the enormous energy and release that is communicated
by those who are engaged in healing people. You cannot be into
healing and not be life-affirming. Obviously there can be bad
practitioners or practitioners who become diverted, even in terrible
ways, from their vocation to heal. But, in so far as people are
genuinely seeking to heal others, it is a clear demonstration and
model of what being life-affirming is like. I am using the term life-
affirming as a way of briefly summing up the whole range of life-
values. In all our living and actions we have the choice over and
over again to affirm life or deny it. I think of stories I have read of
people in situations of utter extremity, for example in concentration camps, who have acted in a life-giving way. Sometimes that
has meant not only putting other people first but even being willing
to risk and sacrifice yourself. This is an extraordinary contra-
diction. Jesus referred to it in his teaching and lived it out in his
death. People who are committed to being life-affirming sometimes
believe that it is better to lose your own life than to take another
person's. Sometimes it seems right to risk everything in an attempt
to see right prevail. Most of us, for much of the time, settle for
much less. But some people display an astonishing resilience and
heroism as they strive to be faithful to this way of living.

5 Give humans acceptance and compassion, justice and peace

Acceptance means being open to what is different and thereby being willing, through standing in other people's shoes and through listening, to be sensitive and responsive to the other person or group. Acceptance also means, contrary to those who fear syncretism, a real concern for the truth. To accept diversity is not to set aside a concern either for the truth you yourself live by or for the search after truth as such. Indeed I find that the sheer fact of being challenged by different ways of thinking, living, valuing actually sharpens my keenness to understand as best I can what the truth is. Acceptance, for me, includes making a clear distinction between being faithful to what you yourself believe and practise and the desire to learn from other people. I do not mean we hold on to what is most precious to us without allowing it to be questioned and that we only dialogue with peripheral and unimportant items on our agendas. I mean rather that it is possible to hold to the essentials of your own faith whilst genuinely allowing your growing understanding of other systems to challenge what you value. The one point at which I believe we have to stick is that we should not be tolerant towards people and groups who themselves are intolerant or who seek to dominate. If you reach the point of realizing that the other person or group is not only concerned to show you the best of their system or even wishes to convert you to it, but actually regards all you stand for as rubbish, then the possibility of acceptance flies out of the window. In the same way you cannot be accepting of people who are using violence against you.

Acceptance, like compassion, justice and peace, is all to do with seeing the worth of humans both as individuals and their interdependence. There is enough in the world contrary to it. There is so much that rubbishes people. There is such power used to take wealth and privilege for the few by denying our mutual dependence and by ignoring the suffering of those who pay the price of exploitation.

The life-values point to the importance of compassion. When in doubt, as a colleague of mine puts it, be generous, be gracious, be compassionate. Straightforward love and care for people has its obvious individual witnesses. We see it also in people who work to care for the dying, in the hospice movement, in so many community self help projects around the world, in emergency relief where there is war, and in caring for people with AIDS. One teacher writes of disinterested compassion and by so doing reminds us that what matters is not what we feel but what we do in answer to the need.

I see such compassion in the daily service of some of the people I have worked with over the years. In the unending minutiae and routine of community work with people who are at the breaking points in our society. I know of it with people who have worked for years with vagrant alcoholics, and I contrast their practical compassion with the embarrassment I always felt when someone came to my door begging, or that I feel even now when people stop me in the street and ask for money. Our sympathy, empathy, our ability to see things from other viewpoints and our ability to act as though it were happening to us, these mark compassion. I remember years ago a near neighbour needing to get into hospital because she kept attempting suicide. I was on the phone to a doctor trying to get her admitted (and out of my hair!) and I found myself shouting down the phone, 'If it were happening to your child you would do something about it.' The life-values are also to do with justice and peace. These words fit well together. Much has been written about the biblical word for peace, the word *shalom*. It is a peace which is total and a peace which is to do with the coming in of God's Kingdom when all are human and all are free at last. I remember occasions over the years with brothers and sisters from South Africa and Namibia. I have stood silent and in tears as they have sung for freedom. I have stood there, with all my personal opposition to the use of violence, and felt at one with their cause against damnable cruelty and generations of injustice. We have to care and act as best we can. It runs from, to give simple examples, not buying South African goods as a form of protest to campaigning against weapons, local rate-capping or some very local community issue. It means acting as though it were happening to us. And in Britain with the inner cities, the ethnic minority communities, the gap between the North and South, the gap between the employed and the unemployed, the awful gap between the poor and the rich in comfortable Britain, it means accepting that it is happening to us and not to them.

These life-values and this way of being human is all about collaboration, participation, interdependence, community. It is what Christians mean by fellowship and it is what some political believers mean by solidarity. I have seen it over ten years in a Christian project for racial justice which used a partnership model to enable black and white people to co-operate and work together within the churches. I have seen it in our own small multi-racial church. It is about a style of leadership which is not authoritarian. It is about a style of practice that is to do with sharing power in an open and genuine way. It is vulnerable and can be easily spoilt by people who want power for themselves. If you are to follow through in working for acceptance, compassion, justice and peace you have to develop real skills. All to do, Jesus said, with being wise and wary as serpents and innocent as doves.

6 Face hard decisions truthfully

We live with constant choices in a world of compromise, conflict, violence. It is extremely hard to be consistent and it is, for most of us, impossible to get it right all the time. But we must face hard decisions truthfully.

We may ask why humans are so destructive and so self destructive. The answer in terms of human sin and social disintegration is simply to give another description rather than an explanation. But, both in personal terms and in socio-political terms, we sometimes have to make hard choices. As a friend of mine puts it, there are some hard lumps to swallow.

What on earth does it mean to be life-affirming and all the rest of these life-values for a black person in South Africa? What do love, justice and peace mean in Ireland, or the Middle East, or between Iran or Iraq, or in any of the disputes stretching into history and stretching into the future? We have to try to go in the direction of that which affirms and leads to peace with justice.

People sometimes suggest that it is one thing to hold a view of morality in private and another to have to make decisions in the real world, as they say, in public. For this reason some people do not risk the compromise of public decision making. Some people operate with two fairly distinct value systems. I think this is mistaken for two reasons. First we need to find ways of dealing with social, economic and political conflicts and realities in some way that does not depend only on the use of power or the use of violence.

Secondly, if the only people who are willing to accept public leadership are people who do not mind deceit, corruption, coercion and worse, then as societies we are in a lot of trouble. This also means recognizing the effect that such decision-making has on the person. I will not list all the scandals and all the chicanery which have led to the ruin of so many of 'the president's men' in all the countries of the world and within all the different systems. It is hard to be truthful in situations of power when choices are always complex and rarely between good and evil. It is hard, but as is witnessed by the lives of so many people, it is possible. The first lie, the first deception, the first attempt to break or remove an opponent are the decisions to be resisted. I see within this complicated situation two signs of encouragement. I believe we should not only increase our hope by looking where significant change has already taken place but we should work hard to understand what caused the change to take place. We need to understand better how conflict and change happen whether it be through the work of local mediation and reconciliation centres or through the work of those concerned with development or peace studies at international level.

We should also look at change which is brought about by non-violent methods. Such methods seem to be in line with the life-values I am advocating. Certainly, if Jesus' death in itself has any lasting significance, part of that significance is surely to do with his non-violent and even self-sacrificing response to evil. Obviously this is extremely difficult. But I believe that we should strive for every possible alternative before violence. And, as those who undertake violence in a just cause know better than I, it may seem the only way but it includes evil means and leads to some bitter harvests.

I think it is vital to see that being life-affirming and non-violent does not lead us into the impasse which critics suggest is unavoidable. Such behaviour does not mean being weak, always giving in or giving way, being pushed around. It does not make people losers. When I think about some of the serious quarrels I have had with people or when I think of some of the sustained conflicts that have happened within my work I am aware that in trying to be life-affirming and non-violent I am using a complex range of strategies and skills. This means that, whatever the conflict, I try to care about the person and, by neither immediately retaliating, nor immediately taking it personally I try to defuse the situation. I suppose I let people have two free shots. Given that the dispute continues, whether I or the other person caused it, I then try neither to respond in a threatening manner nor to attack or seek to belittle the other person. Then, and I think this is hard to do, I would try to be the one who makes the move to solve the conflict and resolve the situation. An important part of this involves using other people to help sort out the truth of what is happening, leaving people with room to manoeuvre rather than aggressively backing them into a corner. If the conflict can be solved, then there is the follow up task of trying to establish a reasonable relationship in which the hurt is not thought of and the bruises no longer are felt. This is not a complete list. It is simply an indication that we are committed to complex personal and intergroup skills which are all to do with mediation, conflict resolution, and forgiveness.

Such a way is difficult and extraordinary. At times, just like anyone else, you get to the end of your tether and that is when I get my machine gun out and shoot the bastards! The disciples asked Jesus how many times they should forgive and the answer was . . . many times. I have found, with just a few exceptions, that solutions can be found. This neither means that all wrongs are forgotten nor that I do not hurt other people. It means that the direction I aim to go and the skills I try to develop are all about being non-violent.

Most of us make our hard decisions at personal level. Is it life-affirming to have a vasectomy or to use contraceptives? Many of us would say, 'Yes', yet a major part of the church still says 'No'. Is it ever right to have an abortion? Can a marriage survive one partner's unfaithfulness? Can a family survive unemployment? How do you react when your twenty-year old children want to sleep with their partners on holiday? How do you react when your child brings home a black friend, a gay friend, a friend from a different religious faith? These situations are all commonplace. I see and find useful these life-values because they provide two things which are of some help in making such difficult choices. They provide a general direction. They offer a sufficiently imaginative range of concepts and feelings to encourage flexibility, conversation, negotiation, all within an overriding concern for people as people.

7   Take sides with the poor

I have learned over a number of years that the only people who argue that taking sides is wrong (un-English or un-Christian) are the people who are so entrenched in their own privilege and their own position that they can best defend it by claiming neutrality. Through my work I have been involved in at least two very hard long-term campaigns, one for racial justice and the other for justice for the poor in Britain and the world. I have been surprised to learn just how resilient, devious and violent people can be in defending their own territory and their own positions. I was naive not to realize it before, but I did not. Now I know, as a slogan puts it, that to do nothing is to take sides. The life-values I am describing push us to take sides with those whose lives are most denied.

It seems to me incontrovertible that the Bible account places, as do other religions at their best, a particular responsibility upon the faithful for the needy, the widows, the orphans, the strangers and aliens, the poor, the outcasts of society. The message runs through the biblical account and has been well documented. Indeed some Gospel scholars believe that Jesus' message to the poor was his most revolutionary and radical contribution because he regarded such as being within the Kingdom of God's grace. I turn to the Gospels directly in this, not because I feel myself on unsure ground, but precisely because the argument about interpretation has to be won. We are called, according to the way of Jesus and, to use the language of Christians in Latin America, to take a preferential option for the poor.

This is scandalous. It goes against all that our society is about and all that our society worships. It flies in the face of what is normally called sense and certainly in the face of what in the short term is seen as self-interest. But it is the right way because we belong together, because we are to show compassion, and because so often

the poor remain poor because we have placed that burden on them
through our individual, corporate and national greed.

I mentioned my own experience in the inner city and on issues
of racial justice. I find I have to take sides in that equally complicated area of women's liberation. My personal hunch is that,
within all the movements for liberation, women's liberation has the
greatest power to change the world. I think this is because women
form the largest single group who are oppressed and disadvantaged.
And I think so because, to our shame, many who work for liberation in South Africa or for black people or for minority rights or
for religious rights do not themselves treat women as equal partners. It is an extraordinary and entrenched evil which, especially
in world terms, places women firmly amongst the poor.

It is a terrible fact that, for all our obvious advances and capa-
bility to provide for people, so many of the world's people remain
in such utter and appalling need. It is even worse to see how often
it is women and children who carry the weight of deprivation. I
read that if there is to be any hope of the world's poor becoming
self-sufficient and independent then we must work to strengthen
the arm of the poor especially so that they will be able to stand up
to those, including us, who in fact exploit them. Such self-reliance
will only be born out of compassionate action and clinical planning.

Three things remain to be mentioned at this point. Part of what
it means to be a human being is to do with our capacity to cry for
other people. If we are always unmoved, if no one's circumstances
or death diminishes us, if we can always find reasons to remain
untouched, then there is something lacking in us as human beings.
This is true whether we see it on TV in dying children, or in the
circumstances of those we know, or in requests for help from total
strangers. If we are never moved, if we are always calculating and
never generous, if we always leave it to others, we are the worse
for that.

I also think part of our humanity is to do with some sense of
fairness and even-handedness. I have thought about this a great
deal. Why should it matter so much that other people's circumstances and need touch me? Why, using the word poor to cover a
whole range of human needs and despair, why should the poor of
the world be our concern? I am sure there are many answers to do
with self-interest and social stability. But I think I see our ability

to treat others in a fair, just and even handed way as one of the
fundamental marks of our humanity.

Finally, our conduct towards the poor is a mark not only of our
compassion and our concern for justice but also of our understanding of our common humanity. Let me explain again in a personal
way. Centuries ago there were bitter wars between Lancashire and
Yorkshire and now all that remains, well almost all, is a certain
rugged hostility about cricket. Millions have died in European wars
and now we are in a European Community. America and the Soviet
Union with their allies and dependents face each other with weapons
of potential mutual destruction now the Berlin wall has come
down. The circle of privilege for many chosen people is always
put to the test at the point where it meets other communities.
Maybe if the world can find a large enough heart and sufficient
political will to address the problems of the world's poor we shall
indeed, at last, understand that we are in fact one family. As I
write the words I see the face of one of my black colleagues, a
senior woman leader in the church. She says with passion, whether
about racism in Britain, apartheid in South Africa or the hungry of
the third world, 'There is only one race, the human race.'

8   Belong to a community of faith

I do not mean it is equally life-enhancing to belong to the Nazi
party, the National Front or the Red Brigade as it is to join a religious organization. But I do know that people find fulfilment and
satisfaction in many communities beyond the church and I want to
affirm that.

It is important for people to belong to more human institutions
than simply the family. There are of course many examples that
are not to do with faith but are nonetheless creative. But in my
experience of a variety of communities of faith there is something
very attractive and very creative in belonging. Such a community
may be stifling and some young people may have to escape. But I
think that it is right to try to practice and pursue our life-values
within communities of faith simply because they include those who
are addressing the same issues.

Conservative forms of religion, of all kinds, believe above all in unchanging systems. To belong is to believe and to accept the tradition and the teaching. The Christian church and many other religions have usually coped with reformation by accepting divisions and splits. But it is clear that there are some parts of the church which expect reform and indeed regard such reform as renewing, whilst other parts of the church are committed, in practice, to being doctrinaire and dogmatic. Of course any group or system has the right to expect a degree of compliance and conformity. What I personally think makes the difference is whether or not a church welcomes new ideas and new ways. Whether it sees such as stretching the church to the limits or with Jesus constantly looks for signs of the new life which he expressed as new wine needing new wine skins.

Belonging and joining in is also important. I am sure that most people stay within a Christian congregation because, however understood and however articulated, they feel at home in it. I see that we have to be guarded in the loyalty we give to the church as to all human institutions. I recognize that in saying this I part company with those Christians who see the church as unique amongst human organizations. But I will stick to that. This is not out of an overblown view of my own importance or even an excess of individualism but it is because I think the credal statement that 'Jesus is Lord' has to be taken very seriously. It means to me that the life-values which are consistent with and derived from the way of Jesus must always come first. Always they stand, when necessary, over against family, kith and kin, nation and even the church.

The church has to wrestle with questions of truth and I think that the church has found this increasingly difficult. It was difficult in the days of Western missionary endeavour when the church misjudged the right relation between faith and culture. It is difficult as the church seeks to relate to all the varieties which make up the pluralism I have been describing. I think the life-values of being life-affirming are especially hard to work out in relation to our faith when it comes to questions of truth. Clearly Christians deal with this in different ways. Let me give examples in the form of three questions:

– How can a Christian person of faith authentically live in a secular society? Can we be secular Christians?

– How can a Christian person of faith hold that faith positively in dialogue with other world faiths, and can we value and learn from each other?

– How can a Christian person of faith be loyal to the affirmation that 'Jesus is Lord' in a world of power politics, and can we pursue justice, peace and love in a violent world?

I would argue that being life-affirming means that we have both to care rigorously about what is true and false within our own system and faith, and to treat others with respect. Put over simply but truly it is always wrong to kill people because you disagree with what they believe and practice. So simple, and yet the world is littered with the corpses and martyrs of such rivalry. But it is consistent with these life-values both to be supported and surrounded by a particular faith community and yet have true respect and regard for other people of faith in theirs.

I do not want to under-estimate the importance of personal devotion or public worship either as times of breakthrough or as peak experiences. Indeed I know some believers regard such occasions as the centre not only of faith but of life. There are moments in Pentecostal worship as a whole congregation sways in prayer and song, there are moments as the bread and wine are given out in eucharist, there are moments in preaching or in informal worship when people find their way through to faith and meaning. This is not to do with what you might call the internal life and affairs of the church: its order, regulation, authority or its attempts to find agreement, within its divided groups, on matters of baptism, eucharist or ministry. No, this is the point at which, for some people often, and for some of us sometimes, the Christian faith becomes a doorway to reality and the effect is felt in our daily ordinary lives.

For the Christian, the local church can be a way of affirming these life-values. Through membership in it, through worship, through the action and service of the church, through seeking to affirm your faith to other people, through sharing your faith in dialogue and apologetics there is encouragement to find a way through.

Although there are many kinds of institutions and communities which are valid and helpful I have found communities of faith to be a crucible in which I have learned about interdependence and sharing. I think back to the church I was brought up in within Lancashire Methodism with all its distinctive cultural overtones, its activities, its families, its liveliness. I think of churches to which I have belonged since. Some have been arid and killed off by internal strife or an almost pathological resistance to change. Others, small and large, have been clusters of groups within which people have been able to test out and learn what it means to be human in community. I think also of people I have got to know who seek to live in intentional communities and I have often been surprised by the vigour of their individuality and the strength of their vocations. In all of them, with all their varieties, I have learned the dangers of any system which emphasizes individuality at the cost of interdependence or community, at the cost of denying personal identity.

9 Be faithful to Jesus

I said quite a lot about Jesus in an earlier section and I do not need to repeat it. I cannot explain or sort out where my life-values are derived from my life experiences and where they come from the Jesus of the Gospels. Both have always been real for me. Their interaction has made me what I am.

This does not mean that all Christians follow Jesus in the same way. Some find Jesus within the teaching of the church and within the church's sacraments. Such Christians fuse the historical Jesus and the Christ of faith with the sacramental Christ whose presence is firmly set within the ritual and confession of the church. Others make a history-crossing link between his death and their own lives and relationship within God. They see a significance in his death and resurrection which leads them to see personal salvation as depending upon faith in the Jesus who alone puts people right with God. Still others unite in some sense the teaching about the Risen Christ with the teaching about the Holy Spirit and find their daily experience of God best described as renewal by the Holy Spirit. But such an experience, both within Pentecostalism and within charismatic renewal, follows on from conversion and rebirth in Jesus.

A great deal of Protestant teaching and much Christian devotion speak of Jesus in a much more contemporary and personal way. The affirmation of faith that Jesus is risen becomes a way of describing present experience. The witness to the gift of the Holy Spirit to the early church becomes a witness to the Spirit-filled content of present experiences. Without denying the truths to which I understand such beliefs are pointing I must say that this is not what I experience. Maybe it is possible to unite the Jesus of history and the risen Jesus with the very fabric of human life as we know it. Maybe it is right for us as Christians to speak of human existence being shot through with the reality of Jesus in the same way that we speak of existence being filled with the glory of God. But we are then into a way of speaking which operates within its own rules and which has pulled back to something different from the Jesus of the Gospels. The New Testament itself shows how developments took place in the understanding of the church about Jesus. Clearly they were interpretations, since Jesus was dead. But throughout the centuries, and in all the changing descriptions made in lives of Jesus, and through all the many attempts to explain the significance of his death all Christians believe that in some fundamental sense individuals have personally to make a commitment to Jesus. The model of a rabbi or guru accepting a disciple and follower has become the model of a person being turned round, converted, repenting. Somehow Jesus has become a focus and a catalyst through which people become new people: their enlightenment (satori), self-realization, salvation from sin, is triggered by Jesus.

So many things come to mind. Moments in Bible study at our church and with other groups when a passage has been made relevant or when a person has been enlivened in commenting on a Gospel passage. I think of people I have seen come to faith. I think of my own journey and, whatever the doubts and faith, the way I keep on coming back to the Gospels of Jesus. Though any Greek language I ever knew has faded and though too many of my books are old and I have read too little of what is new and fresh, still I wrestle, as so many others have done, with this Jesus. I cannot say, as some can, that this Jesus has recognizably entered my life and experience as a supernatural presence. But his life, teachings, death and resurrection, as attested within the Gospels, have been a constant source of motivation and formation of all that is the most human in me. Of all the books I have read, of all the creative people whose work has fired or angered or enthused me, I remain stuck with this Jesus of Nazareth.

Sometimes I try again to read the Gospels of Jesus as though for the first time. I know this is impossible, but I take a deep breath, step back, and try to put down all the years of study and familiarity. I try to read these four books and their relatively few number of pages with fresh eyes. I look for what is most obvious and striking in the four accounts, I wonder why some of us find them so compelling and other people dismiss them almost out of hand. I see the facts of his life and the religious witness surrounding him, I see the attempts to express his identity and mission. I see his teaching about God's Kingdom and his call to people to enter it by repentance. I see his healings, the few miracles, his clash with religious people, I see the disciples and the way of life to which they are called. And above all, almost between the lines, and running through the teaching and actions I see all the people Jesus met. I especially notice how they were among the outcasts, the sick, the insane, the widows, the orphans, the prostitutes, the tax collectors, the poor. I see, as one writer has put it so vividly, Jesus in bad company and I see the salvation history of Israel before it, and the faith of the church after it, trying to deal with this reality which was at once as scandalous and significant as his execution. For all the critical questions, all the difficulties, the contradictions, the complexity, I feel and believe that the truth that comes through, as of Jesus, is consistently and radically, root and branch, affirming of people. It especially affirms those who others see as being worthless and it sets them within God's Kingdom of righteousness and peace.

10 Stay restless

One of the early fathers of the church said that our hearts are restless until they find their rest in God.

Religion over the centuries and over the world has wrestled with some ancient and ultimate questions. In many parts of the world and for millions of people those questions are still answered and met through faith in God. It is quite breathtaking to see the way people are enriched and formed by the practice of their faith, by their own private devotion, and by the public practice of their religion. I see this all around in the religious faiths and systems of our world. I see it in our Christian faith. Some people are deeply satisfied by their faith, others are not and leave or never join, others are not but stay or try a different faith.

Having been born into a Christian family, I found the idea, let alone the experience, of the absence of God a strange one. And yet I have learnt over the years, through my constant work within the church but in secular culture, that most people live with a declared faith in God which hardly affects how they behave at all. I, in contrast, affirm my faith in God somewhat hesitantly but find she pushes me around all the time! When I consider, as a seventeenth-century philosopher taught me to do, that I am alive now rather than then, and here rather than there, I am rather knocked sideways. It does astonish me. It does make me grapple, in a way that saying I believe in God curiously does not, with the sheer fact that I am responsible for my life. If the God of the gaps has gone and we have to be believers in a world come of age, then there is a real shock to the believer's system to discover that I am on my own between life and death and this is it.

My life-values, through my experiences and through critical reflection within the church, remain, to use shorthand, in a post-Darwinian scientific world. Part of me feels that I have explored that world so far that I have put my faith in God at risk. I remember a teacher warning sternly and philosophically that some might have to risk becoming atheists for the sake of the Kingdom of God: which was, in so far as I understood it at the time, and certainly is as I understand it now, a way of saying that you can go down some roads so far that there is nothing left to do but to fall off the cliff. It is also to do with the idea that we only get answers to the questions we ask, the problem being how to get at the right questions about God.

Some Christians and people of faith talk as though God were on the other end of a telephone and that their lives are directed in a one to one causal sense.

Other Christians and other people of faith witness to a living faith in God. It is all to do with a conscious relationship with an independent being who, though distinct from the world, operates and communicates within it. For Christians this can be expressed quite differently. Some emphasize the grace of God through Jesus and have a living experience which they see as having transformed their lives. Others, to give one other example, lean heavily upon the church and its sacraments to provide the consistent experience of the presence of God. I find many such people live with consistently gracious ways. Through them they witness to a power beyond themselves. I have to say that, hard as it is to admit, this is not what is happening to me. But staying restless for God means several things which are extremely important and which are my way of expressing my faith in God.

I belong with those people who say 'we believe in God'. I believe, both from within the classic arguments about the existence of God and from within my own experience, that whatever reality human life and existence holds is of God. I believe that, whatever I do not know about the origin or destiny of myself or the universe, it is full of sense and meaning. I believe that Jesus' life, death and resurrection are, for me, a wholly engrossing and demanding way through to God. I see within our human experience and within our universe that which is authentic rather than counterfeit. I see that which is truly gracious and to do with giving. And I see in people above all that which pulls me out beyond our humanity. There is so much that I do not know or understand. There is so much to be said, as many religions do say, about what God is not. It is so hard in a world and society of such unbelief. But within the church I do believe in the God of Abraham and Isaac and Jacob, I do believe in the God of Jesus, I do believe in the God to whom so many religious faiths point. And, outside the world of such faith, I do believe, in a way that I can hardly begin to express, that the stuff and fabric and energy of life itself is more than itself. That words like grace, forgiveness, being, purpose are not just casually right but are, in some utter way, at the very centre and heart of being itself.

And so things do happen to me which have a feel of God and of Jesus. I know I am too restless, too arguing, questioning, doubting to ever be wholly a person of faith. Though I know enough to guess this could happen to me just to show I had it wrong! But there are moments for myself, in people I love, within the life of the church to which I belong, which are so disproportionately surprising, extraordinary and gracious that I have a sense not just of self-transcendence but of being transcended. I find it easier to describe such times in terms of mystical experience than in terms of the language of salvation. But when such times come, as they have in the past, and as I hope they will in the future, I am amazed that I ever doubt the meaning, sense and purpose of life. I know deep within me that it is all one. I know that the life-values, as I call them, take us in the right direction. Absolutely it is right to affirm life. Absolutely it is right to resist evil. Totally it is vital to struggle and hunger to see right prevail so that humans may be human. And meanwhile the God to whom this points has already moved on.

I am sure of one thing. It is that anyone who has come within, to use a very human expression, even a million miles of the most gentle or passing sense of the presence of God will care more about the tears of a child than about defending their own vision of God.

In our living room we have a copy of a painting. I have seen the original a few times. It is an abstract and stylized lane with its greens, yellows and blacks. There is a path overhung with wonderfully and thickly painted foliage. The path disappears through a central, almost circular tunnel and, unlike the underpasses in the city, it looks strangely welcoming. Its light shows a way through.

For some people all talk of what is important and precious is God-talk and from within the faith that is right. But for me, starting from where I have started, living as I have lived, sharing with a church as I have, staying restless for God comes a long, long way into the journey. As I look hardest at the uncertainty and puzzle of life, as I remember astonishing moments of intensity and wholeness, as I see so much change then I try to begin to be strong enough to get to the deep things of life. I know I have hardly begun.

11 Create the future

I began with sharing what is important and precious to me. I tried to uncover some of the personal experiences and raw materials which led to me speaking of the life-values by which I want to live. I set all of this within the critical reflection of Christian faith and tried to take a step in the right direction of doing theology in context. All of this led me to persist with the life-values and their application in practice. And now, having given ten answers to the question how, let me stop here.

The dedication uses the phrase for our children and our children's children and it comes from a prayer I often use.

I began with our children and I stop with the future. If life-values and the way of Jesus mean anything, they mean it not only for me now but for others now and in the future. If what is life-affirming now is true then it will be of worth in the future. People sometimes say, 'Oh it doesn't matter, I won't be around to see it.' But in fact it does matter. The way of living I am pointing to is a way for humanity which seeks to be not only for our time and place but truly for the earth and its people.

Guessing what the future will be like becomes more difficult, not less, when you live in a world which is constantly changing. Three things stretch tantalizingly ahead of us.

In the summer of 1987, so the newspapers said, the five billionth baby was born – that is the 5000 millionth. Demographers are saying that, whilst in 1650 the population was half a billion, by the year 2050 it could be ten billion, that is, twice what it is now. Startling as these facts are in terms of what they mean about the number of young people alive now compared with any previous time in history, or how they will be fed, maybe the most amazing of all is that the population of Europe will be such a very small proportion of the world's population. So the question of how to be human individually and collectively becomes desperately pressing when the numbers are so vastly increasing and when our own most precious and important understanding is set in a global context.

Overlapping this fact is the question of whether or not we humans can sustain the earth. The question of whether or not we shall destroy the earth and each other through war and nuclear war has been the grim new fact of my generation. The related questions of how we harvest and nurture the world's resources and how we cope with their unending waste and destruction, often in the name of short term profit, will undoubtedly be part of the hard reality of the future.

The third example is the strangest of all. I read about science's exploration and investigation of space with real interest. On one level it is technical and beyond understanding. On another level, the night we stayed up to watch men walk on the moon seemed not only historical but also a promise of what lay ahead. The discoveries and theories about stars, planets, life forms, even within our own galaxy raise the fundamental questions as to whether or not we humans are alone in the universe.

Our children will meet these and other questions which as of now I cannot even frame. But I cannot imagine, I cannot even in the furthermost reaches of my imagination, imagine that they can live in the future without finding ways through to life-values which are important and precious to them.

I have not quoted sources for what I have written, though I am grateful to so many people for what they have lived, said and written. But one favourite story comes to me at this point. It comes from another time and place, but it hits accurately at what I have been attempting to do.

A Confucian came to a Zen Master to be initiated. The Master quoted Confucious: 'Do you think I am holding something back from you? Indeed I have held nothing back.' After an exchange between the two the enquirer was troubled. But later, when the two were walking in the mountains, with the perfume from the wild laurel in the air, the Master asked the Confucian if he could smell it. When the Confucian agreed the Master said: 'There . . . I have kept back nothing from you.'